D1296627

TO MY SISTER GEORGINA,

AND TO MY GRANDMOTHERS CONCHA AND CECILIA

Cocktail Cuisine

TONY BOTELLA

PROJECT DIRECTOR
Francisco Marfull

ART DIRECTOR
Xavier Corretjé

PHOTOGRAPHY
Manel Huete

TRANSLATION
Michael Debbane

PROJECT COORDINATOR
Cèlia Pujals

LAYOUT
René Palomo

PRODUCTION DIRECTOR
Luis Miguel Calvo

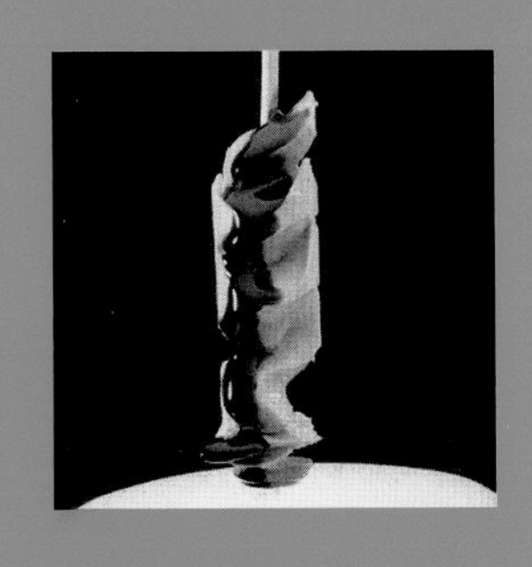

UNITS OF MEASUREMENT

ABBREVIATIONS USED IN THE RECIPES

gal.	gallon
in.	inch
lb.	pound
oz.	ounce
qt.	quart
tbsp.	tablespoon
tsp.	teaspoon

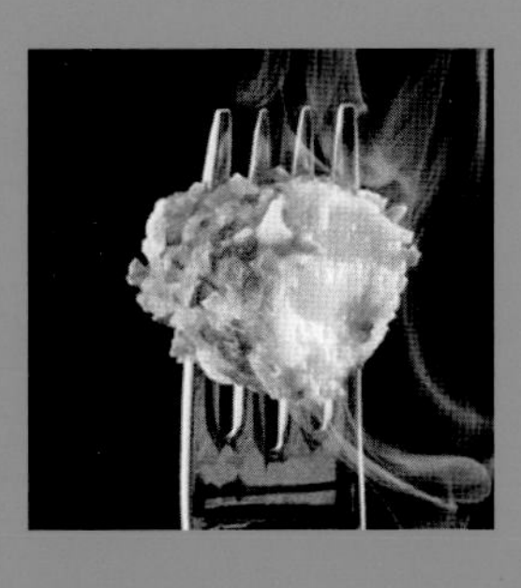

Foreword

When Tony showed me the hors d'œuvres he was creating, my first surprise came with the realization that this delicate cylinder resembling a strange, unattainable material for non-initiates like myself was in fact only bread, simple bread...

In my opinion, a good chef is one who knows the basics well—something that sounds obvious but for some reason is less common than it may seem. I do not usually enjoy sophistication in my daily life, nor do I in the kitchen. That is why what Tony offers in this book is doubly valuable. Many of these works of art are made of bread, tomato, cured meat... Why make something sophisticated when it is already good in itself?

Some seem like pieces of silverworking, though behind them is not sophistication but much imagination, which is very different—because only imagination turns par-baked bread into a glorious canapé.

Another thing I like about this book is that it reclaims a more natural way to eat. Botella wants to recapture seasonal flavors and eat what nature gives us. In a time when the food industry allows us to eat figs in January and asparagus year-round, Tony would like us to learn to value the ingredients available in their prime, not before or after.

I always lived in Barcelona, which is perhaps why one of the things that surprised me when I arrived in Madrid (where I've lived for almost 8 years) was the custom in virtually any bar to include a tapa with a drink. I loved the idea of transforming a simple soft drink into a small surprise appetizer. Not only for the generous and hospitable gesture, but because the aperitif is the course we who love to eat enjoy the most. What's more, the appetizer is sometimes better than the rest of the meal, because it is more social and allows us to change company and conversation with ease when we find ourselves with the wrong cocktail group.

In any case, the appetizer is full of substance, though for the taste buds and the stomach it would be better to have less. That said, we tend to be very indulgent with aperitifs. Although what is served may not be a delicacy, we are usually left feeling that the snack was fantastic.

The only risk of the aperitif is that it may spoil the subsequent meal. We must therefore make it precise. The one who enjoys it must avoid succumbing to the extra beer that ruins the moment, to that one unnecessary piece of cheese. And the one who prepares it must create mouthfuls good for savoring but not for eating.

It may sound a bit cliché, but I take great pleasure in saying that Tony and I are what are often called "old friends". I have seen him work in that space that in his house is called the workshop and is bigger than the living room. That sophisticated and professional kitchen that many restaurants would want for themselves is a relatively recent marvel. Before this, Tony had accomplished almost the same with much more primitive tools. Because this is his vocation, Tony already made the basics well: a good rice soup, some good croquettes, a good Spanish tortilla and a collection of inventions that we friends and family have tried without fail in all these years...

I remember him dreaming of a convection oven that would make his very delicate chocolate soufflés rise evenly. Many of our dinners continue to be a proving ground in which Tony obtains information about a new sauce, a new way to fry or a dessert none of us have ever tried.

Today is one for appetizers. Amuse-bouche, tapa, morsel, hors d'œuvre, snack... Finally, I, who knows words better than recipes, only wish to stop looking at the photos and start biting into these morsels. I leave to the experienced reader the pleasure of creating them before tasting them.

LORENZO MILÁ

It gives me great pleasure to present my friend Tony Botella's original book. I know that he has been and always will be a true "Bulliniano"; it is surely this connection that allows me to appreciate and understand his work so well.

This may not be the first time we see miniature cuisine, but it is the first time we come across a book that treats the subject with the importance it deserves and a completely modern focus.

The focus that Tony Botella, a great professional and researcher of gastronomy, puts into all of his creations—small culinary treats that combine traditional and avant-garde cuisine—our Spanish gastronomy with some foreign influence. And all of this is researched and calculated to give these pieces the presence, grace and originality to make them worthy of the best cocktail parties.

Tony rejects the term "miniature cuisine", and not without reason. We are in fact presented with elaborate culinary delights, full-fledged cuisine with full-fledged flavor. As he says, "eating while standing" no longer requires resorting to the bread base omnipresent until recent times in any aperitif consisting of canapés, puff pastries, tartlets and others. And he demonstrates it in this book: his appetizers are fresh, light, hot or cold, liquid or solid, and they are always perfect for turning a cocktail gala into a truly special event. And, in my opinion, what is more important: they can open one's eyes to a new concept, act as inspiration and arouse everyone's creativity to imagine a great deal more...

FERRAN ADRIÀ

To my collaborators

Manel Huete

In appearance, Manel Huete is a 'normal' photographer: he has no piercings, does not dress extravagantly, nor does he lay on the floor in contortionist postures to take a fantastic photo. No, he is simply a family man, a professional photographer with his own studio; a lover of all that is technical, a perfectionist and above all a good professional.

Over the last ten years we have perhaps photographed more than two thousand dishes, still-lifes, buffets and desserts. When we now look through the first photos we did together in the early nineties, we begin to laugh: they were dishes prepared in a basement kitchen, which we brought up in an elevator to an improvised set two floors above. I remember that if the dish was hot, I brought it up hot and didn't even worry about cleaning up the cuts, drizzling certain products with oil so that they shone or looking for the best pieces. It was simple: I would place the plate in front of the lens and he would have to shoot.

With great subtlety and extreme prudence, Manel Huete has always known how to show me my strengths and weaknesses, how to suggest to me what I did well and what I did poorly. He has guided me through all these years, and I think that with time we have 'gelled'—we have come to understand each other and agree on the little details that, according to him, are one of the keys to making a good photo.

He has always supported me and trusted in my potential as a stylist. If today I can presume to know how to dress up an ingredient to make it look good in a photo, it is thanks to him.

The mastery of modifying food for photography, however, is one that we seldom contemplate. In reality, the photography work in this book was the culmination of a goal that we two set for ourselves some time ago: to do the work without chemistry, digital touch-ups, or tricks. We wanted work that was natural, real and clean. If you observe the photographs closely you will note that there is not a single decorative leaf, not one inedible adornment—absolutely nothing but the dish as described in the recipe. This meant many hours of work, and Manel had to put a lot into it.

The natural defects of the ingredients make the work of photographing them with satisfactory results difficult. Nevertheless, we did not want to hide those defects with artificial means. This meant that Manel had to face the inconveniences and resolve them with the use of light, with much enthusiasm and, above all, with great patience and professionalism.

Manel Huete is a great photographer; what's more, he is for me a better person and a better friend.

JUAN MANUEL CLAVERO

Thanks to my work as Gastronomical Adviser of the Paradis Group and as Director of its R + D Department, I had the opportunity to meet a character like Juan Manuel Clavero.

A bachelor who, though he does not show it, has reached his forties. Climber, tai chi instructor, adventurer, cook and, with strong principles, a passionate defender of everything natural.

Juan Manuel Clavero is a mischievous man with strong character, and he is of those cooks who take pleasure in traditional cooking. He likes stews and his face lights up when it comes time to follow a recipe of old. He makes a long face if certain of his habits are altered and he becomes an endearing quick-tempered character fitting for a Walt Disney film, griping aloud about inventions and continuously asking himself: if it has always been done in this way with good results, why should we change it now?

The truth is that he is a great cook and a great friend of mine. And I must admit, he is the one who has always helped me out of rough spots.

Without a word of complaint, and doting on each of the pieces contained in this book, Juan Manuel was one of the people who pushed me most to dare to write a cookbook for professionals.

If not for him, Manel Huete and my wife, this book would not exist.

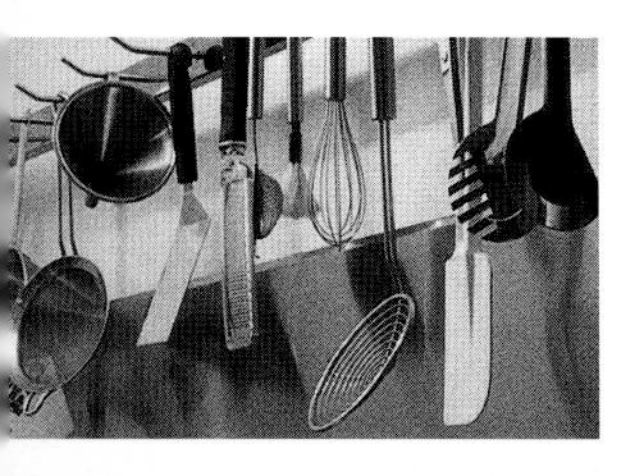

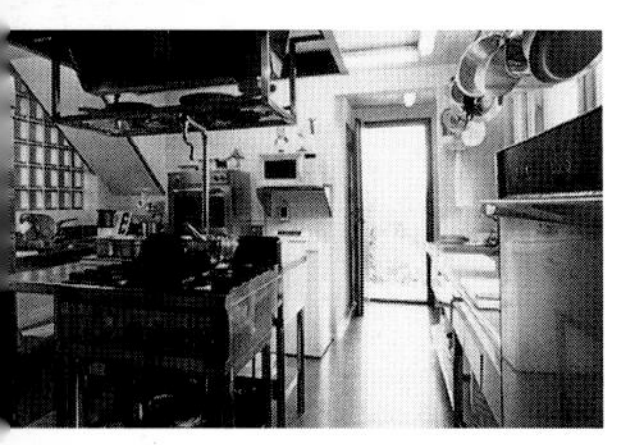

A chef needs a space with the tools and means necessary to be able to do his work. This space is called the kitchen. It is clear that a chef needs a kitchen like a cyclist needs a bicycle. This kitchen can be at the disposal of a dining-room with a serving staff and a schedule—this setup is called a restaurant.

Nonetheless, nowadays professional kitchens can have functions other than producing finished dishes to be served to clients at the usual hours of lunch and dinner. This is the case of my space: a kitchen with no dining room, a place in which dishes and techniques are developed, either for their own sake or by request of a client. In other words, a cooking studio or workshop.

The workshop is situated in my house: that is, it is the house kitchen. Very close to Barcelona, more specifically in Canyet, exists a place that is neither town nor village, nor what is usually construed as a neighborhood. It is a valley with dispersed houses and cottages, and a minuscule urban center. I was born in one of these houses and today, just next door and overlooking the entire valley with the city of Barcelona in the distance, is my home, my studio and my office. It is an office with great picture windows, surrounded by nature and with much natural light. A place in which peace and quiet reign, ideal for relaxing and getting to work, write, draw and put on paper everything which I later develop in the workshop.

The workshop

ZANUSSI
ZANUSSI

LES LOUIS
LES LOUIS
Royal
Royal
Colman's
Mustard
Maldon
Sea Salt

Oriol Balaguer

THE HOW AND WHY OF ITS CREATION

The workshop at first was created for my favorite pastime, the simple act of cooking without any type of influence—without anything or anyone saying, imposing or suggesting anything. To cook without outside rules, enjoying a feeling of boundless freedom, where there is room only for concentration, imagination and the desire for preparations to evoke a special sensation in the few that from time to time sit in the dining room next to the studio. Little by little, there began to appear some demand for my work: professionals in the business requesting consulting, training courses for their employees, menu designs, etc.

Over time, the workshop found its own raison d'être. It is presently a center specialized in consultancy for companies and mainly in the preparation of courses and seminars for professionals. Another of its main activities is the development of the *sous-vide* cooking technique; and in addition, a great passion of mine, food styling.

All of the photos in this book were taken in the workshop. Manel Huete arranged his set in the dining room, and we worked there together.

We also develop home economics projects for magazines as well as culinary producers and other companies related to the food industry.

WHO DOES THE WORK AND HOW

By and large, I work alone. In the attic of the house is the office, where my secretary arranges and puts what comes out of the workshop into words on paper, often stained with one of the ingredients from the recipe in question. However, when the orders reach a certain volume I always count on the unconditional collaboration of Víctor Sánchez, chef and patron of a hotel situated in the heart of the Pyrenees called Mas Tubert. Víctor devours projects and visions and is part of the soul of my workshop. And along with him, names like Víctor Oller, Juan Manuel Clavero and Vicens Arias. These people appear reliably and work with me—they feel at home, they don their chef jackets with astonishing ease and with cutting board and knife in hand ask impatiently:

Tony, what are we doing today?

Evidently, because there are no customers, work tends to be relaxed, chats and debates are on the order of the day, and at 2 o'clock, without fail, we eat. We eat in the kitchen. The comments, laughter and food offer us, on most of the days we spend together, very special moments that, for their lack of stress, contrast with the discipline and respect for a job well done that we demand of ourselves in our profession.

iSi

WHY EAT STANDING UP?

We Catalan chefs have the good or bad custom of telling each other everything. We are bound by a relationship of trust, and we enjoy the freedom of going to one another in search of help and advice. For most of us secrecy has no place. In fact, we take pleasure in sharing our findings, unveiling the new techniques we discover and put into use. Perhaps it seems like a utopian or, at the very least, an idealized situation, but the truth is that companionship between chefs is something real and palpable. Actually, if we analyzed the evolution of inventive Catalan cuisine in recent years, we would find a multitude of examples in which we could guess at the fruit of that collaboration, of that exchange that comes about naturally and unselfishly.

Without a doubt, this way of sharing work and friendship has contributed to the prominence of our country as a point of reference in the culinary world.

Thanks to what I have just 'confessed', the richness of techniques, products and new or revived knowledge has extended to all environments and situations that involve the tasting of food. Until we reach the cocktail hour. Not too long ago, a meal 'standing up' would consist of a more or less varied assortment of canapés, tartlets and snacks, in addition to the classic: fried foods, stuffed olives and ham slices. This was, of course, before the revolution caused by the great innovator of our cuisine (Ferran Adrià, unnecessary to name him) upended this concept as well.

Perhaps it sounds exaggerated to say that in Catalonia the appetizer or cocktail before a menu is almost more important than the menu itself, but it is true that it is at least equally important. A wedding cocktail party can last up to 2 hours. It also has the peculiarity of being eaten standing up.

What type of food to offer for 2 hours that does not produce a sensation of saturation and allows one to sit down afterwards to eat a series of courses, a dessert and a piece of cake? From my point of view, none. But it is true that some are more apt than others. For example, a lettuce leaf or wedge of grapefruit are fresher and lighter than a canapé, a tartlet, pizza, brioche or small sandwich. And in this trivial observation is the key—this is how we uncover the real culprit of the gastronomical revolution in the world of appetizers: flour. Why do I blame my dear, beloved flour? Because it was, traditionally, in various forms and preparations, the support for all food destined for the cocktail. These types of items (i.e. canapés, tartlets, brioches, pizzas, puff pastries, small sandwiches, etc.) presented various problems: on the one hand, they were too filling (something that is sometimes desired, sometimes not) before the copious meal they tended to precede; on the other hand, in more than one case the flour base did not go especially well with the ingredient it supported. And so substitutes began to be sought. The most often used was the bamboo skewer. Following this, the apprehension disappeared and the solutions multiplied: small spoons, glasses, cups and an endless multitude of small recipients including natural elements opened the door for many foods that had had their cocktail gala entry denied because they were poor and ugly, and dressed inadequately besides. Today, with imagination and common sense, they are all invited. Their presence spectacularly enriches the assortment and brings originality to those events with stand-up tasting.

And so that visionary who some years ago imagined a cocktail gala in which, in lieu of a caviar or salmon canapé were offered potatoes with *chorizo*, beef stew, green salad or roasted chicken, was not at all off track. He broke the ice, and there began the revolution.

INDEX 0

STEWS IN A CUP 114

MAKICANAPÉS 148

SPAGHETTI 132

RIBS 156

SPOONFULS 138

ADDITIONAL HORS D'ŒUVRES 174

Note: All terms followed by an asterisk (*) are defined in the glossary (pp. 206-209).

Foie bonbons

Given the nature of foie, it is no mystery that the preparations in this chapter have a certain parallel, as much in form as in base, with chocolate. In fact, the mix that allows us to give shape to foie gras is loosely inspired by the technique for chocolate, though the only thing both ingredients have in common is that they are high in fat. Otherwise, the differences are many. When blended, foie reaches a certain temperature which can cause it to 'break', separate and lose the qualities necessary for preparing it as explained in the following pages.

On the other hand, it is impossible to describe technical processes with precise rises and falls in temperature, since not all livers are the same and their manipulation depends on the quality or even the species of duck. In the technical aside are given some approximate guidelines and a series of visual notes to help in successfully executing this delicate preparation.

The alcohol added to the purée has the function of enhancing flavor, and it can vary according to individual taste, as can the quantities of salt and pepper. Logically, if the maceration in liquid (alcohol) is altered, it is reflected in the texture and behavior of the mix—for that reason, I do not recommend altering the indicated proportion.

Once a good mix is made, the application of the product depends on the individual. I have given most bonbons a relatively simple and minimal treatment: this is the case in those with salt, pepper, nuts, etc. Others are more complicated, like the 'foie bonbons with candied almonds and vinegar'. No doubt a good pastry chef who has mastered the technique of making bonbons could do wonders and far exceed the examples I present in this book. In reality, the goal is to offer a technique—some processes that each one can personalize, put into practice and improve upon so as to finally create his/her own style. I think this can be fun and I am convinced that many will make some fantastic pieces.

THE TECHNIQUE:
MIX FOR FOIE BONBONS

INGREDIENTS

- 2-3/16 lbs. premium quality fresh foie gras
- 2 tbsp. brandy
- 2 tbsp. sweet sherry
- 2 tbsp. white vermouth
- 1 tbsp. salt
- 1 tsp. black pepper

METHOD

1. Chop the foie gras using a knife.
2. Place it in the Thermomix with the rest of the ingredients.
3. Blend at speed level 6 for 1 minute, then at the maximum level for 10 seconds.
4. Check to make sure that there are no lumps, small pieces, etc.

Note: You must take into account the temperature of the foie as well as that of the container in which it is blended—this will directly affect the texture of the mix.

5. Move the mix from the Thermomix to a stainless steel bowl.
6. Refrigerate for a few minutes at 37°F (3°C) before use. If manipulated with a pastry bag, the mix can be refrigerated directly in it.

Chopped foie, ingredients for seasoning and Thermomix container.

Blend at level 6 for 1 minute, then at maximum speed.

Stir with spatula or rubber spatula.

Foie bonbons with pepper

Ingredients (for 20 pieces)

- 3 oz. mix for foie bonbons (p. 27)
- freshly ground black pepper

Method

1. Spoon the mix into a disposable pastry bag with no tip attached.
2. Shape the bonbons by lightly moving the pastry bag back and forth and angling the bag so that they end up wider than they are tall. Finish in a peak.
3. Dust with freshly ground black pepper and freeze.

Serving

1. Allow to thaw at 37°F (3°C).
2. Do not leave at room temperature for longer than 1 hour.

Note: if the mix for foie bonbons is well made (p. 27) the bonbon will maintain its shape for many hours, though after 1 hour the texture will be too soft to pick it up with your fingers (always depending on the room temperature).

Shape the bonbons.

Foie bonbons with nuts and raisins

Ingredients (for 20 pieces)

- 3 oz. mix for foie bonbons (p. 27)
- 20 pistachios
- 20 raisins
- 20 pine nuts

Method

1. Spoon the mix into a disposable pastry bag with no tip attached.
2. Shape bonbons ending in a peak, placing the peak slightly to one side to leave room for the nuts and raisins.
3. Top with one pistachio, one raisin and one pine nut.

Serving

1. Allow to thaw at 37ºF (3ºC).
2. Do not leave at room temperature for longer than 1 hour.

Note: if the mix for foie bonbons is well made (p. 27) the bonbon will maintain its shape for many hours, though after 1 hour the texture will be too soft to pick it up with your fingers (always depending on the room temperature).

Foie bonbons with candied almonds and vinegar

Ingredients (for 10 pieces)

- 1 oz. mix for foie bonbons (p. 27)
- crushed candied almonds
- Forum vinegar* reduction (p. 192)

Method

1. Lay out two PVC strips onto a baking sheet.
2. Place a silicone stencil with rectangle shapes on top and align with the PVC.
3. Spread on the mix for bonbons with a spatula to fill the rectangles.
4. Refrigerate for 30 minutes.
5. Carefully remove the stencil.
6. Cut the PVC strips to separate the resulting foie rectangles.
7. Make into cylinders and attach them with adhesive tape.
8. Use a spatula to close one of the ends off with foie bonbon mix. Freeze.
9. Mix the crushed candied almonds with the Forum vinegar reduction. Spoon into a pastry bag, then fill the cylinders.
10. Cover the other end with foie bonbon mix and freeze.

Note: if you want to add some decoration like that which subtly appears in the photo, you can do it with a knife after step 3. You can mark the bonbons with any desired shape or with fine lines.

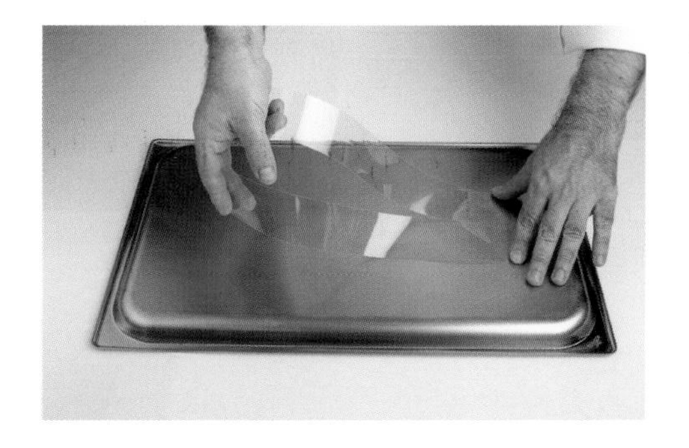

Lay out the PVC strips onto a baking sheet.

Secure them with tape.

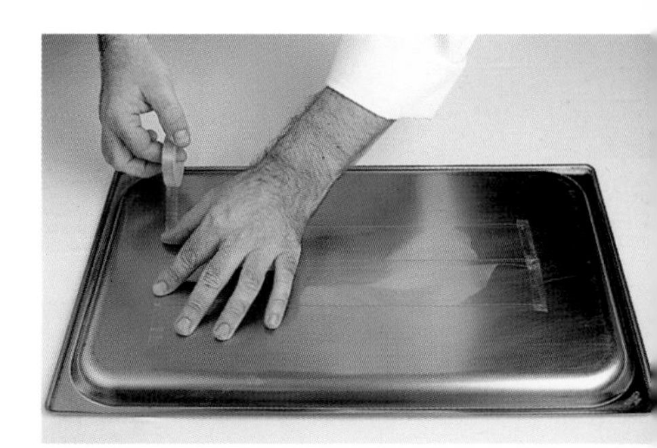

Place the silicone stencil on top of the PVC.

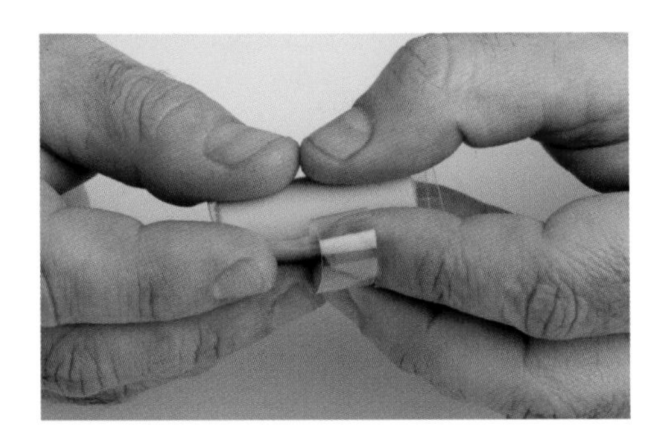

Make the cylinder and attach with adhesive tape.

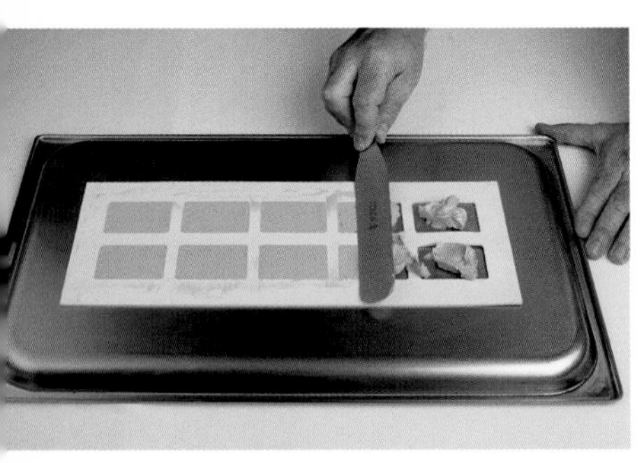

Fill the rectangles completely with the foie mix using a spatula.

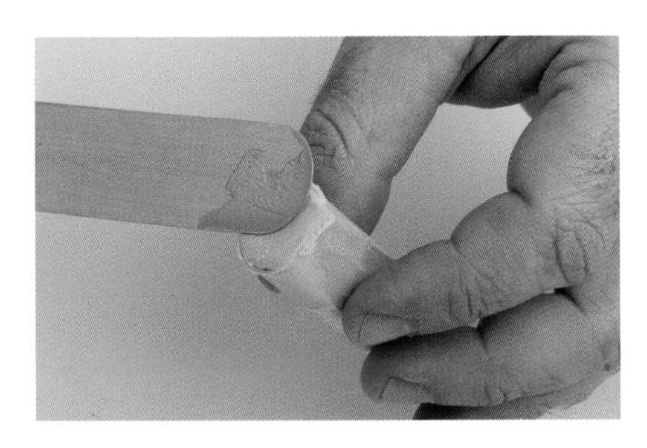

Close one end with the foie mix and freeze.

Lift the stencil when the preparation is cold enough.

Mix the crushed almonds with the vinegar reduction.

Cut the PVC.

Fill the cylinder with the candied almonds and vinegar and close off the end with the foie mix.

SERVING

1. Remove the PVC (it must always be removed immediately after taking the bonbons out of the freezer, never when thawed).
2. Allow to thaw at 37°F (3°C).
3. Remove from the refrigerator and serve immediately.

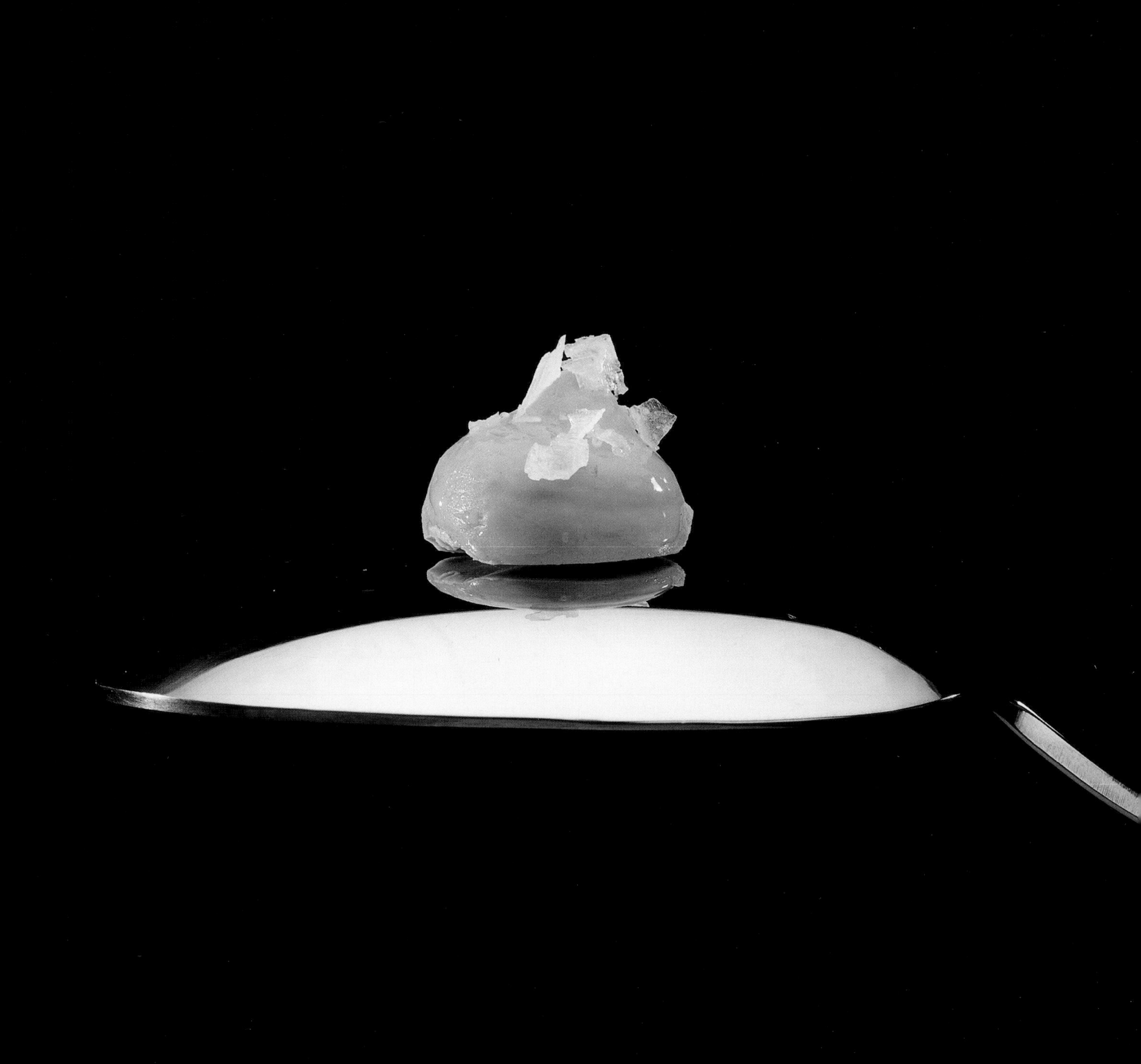

Foie bonbons with salt

Ingredients (for 20 pieces)

- 3 oz. mix for foie bonbons (p. 27)
- Maldon sea salt

Method

1. Spoon the mix into a disposable pastry bag with no tip attached.
2. Shape bonbons ending in a peak.
3. Top with a few Maldon salt crystals and freeze.

Serving

1. Allow to thaw at 37°F (3°C).
2. Do not leave at room temperature for longer than 1 hour.

Note: if the mix for foie bonbons is well made (p. 27) the bonbon will maintain its shape for many hours, though after 1 hour the texture will be too soft to pick it up with your fingers (always depending on the room temperature).

Foie bonbons with licorice

Ingredients (for 20 pieces)

- 3 oz. mix for foie bonbons (p. 27)
- licorice powder (p. 190)

Method

1. Spoon the mix into a disposable pastry bag with no tip attached.
2. Shape bonbons ending in a peak by lightly moving the pastry bag back and forth with progressively smaller movements.
3. Sprinkle a bit of licorice powder on top, then freeze.

Serving

1. Allow to thaw at 37°F (3°C).
2. Do not leave at room temperature for longer than 1 hour.

Note: if the mix for foie bonbons is well made (p. 27) the bonbon will maintain its shape for many hours, though after 1 hour the texture will be too soft to pick it up with your fingers (always depending on the room temperature).

Shape the bonbons.

Sprinkle with licorice.

Foie bonbons "nature" or with balsamic vinegar reduction

Ingredients (for 10 pieces)

- 2-1/2 oz. mix for foie bonbons (p. 27)
- balsamic vinegar reduction (p. 192)

Method

1. Spoon the mix into a disposable pastry bag with no tip attached (cut the end of the bag so that the diameter of the hole is no greater than 3/8 in.).
2. Make PVC cylinders 5/8 in. in diameter and 1-5/8 in. high.
3. Place metal rings onto a non-stick sheet. Place the PVC cylinders inside so that they touch each other and keep each other upright.
4. With the pastry bag, fill the cylinders in the shape of a zigzag.
5. Insert a bamboo skewer into each cylinder as vertically as possible and freeze. Keep the bonbons in the PVC while freezing and storing.

Ingredients and PVC cylinders.

SERVING

1. Take out of the freezer and remove the PVC (it must always be removed immediately after taking the bonbons out of the freezer, never when thawed).
2. Leave "nature" or, with a kitchen "eyedropper", top with a few drops of balsamic vinegar reduction before serving.

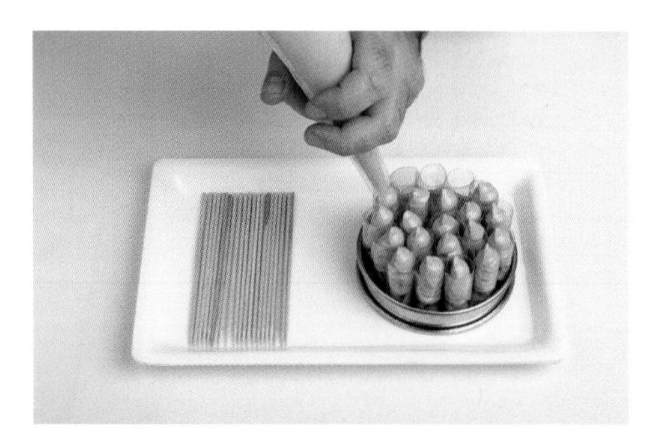

Fill the cylinders.

Insert a bamboo skewer and freeze.

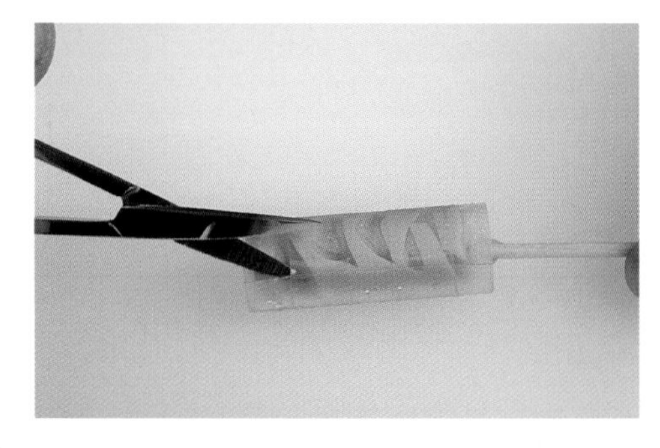

Remove the PVC with the aid of small scissors.

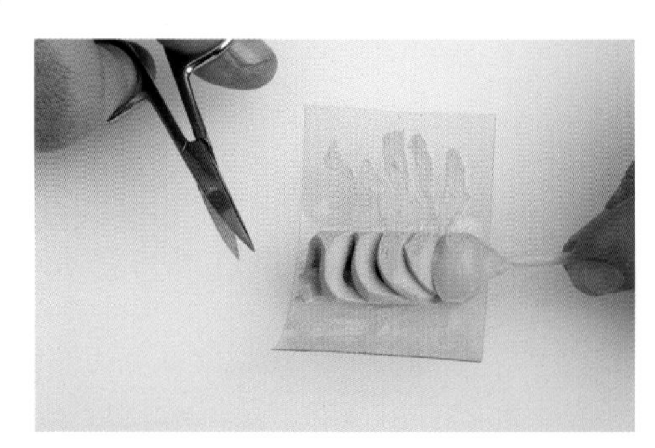

Foie bonbons with orange

Ingredients (for 20 pieces)

- 3 oz. mix for foie bonbons (p. 27)
- orange dust (p. 191)

Method

1. Spoon the mix into a disposable pastry bag with no tip attached.
2. Shape bonbons ending in a peak.
3. Sprinkle some orange dust on top of the peak and freeze.

Serving

1. Allow to thaw at 37ºF (3ºC).
2. Do not leave at room temperature for longer than 1 hour.

Note: if the mix for foie bonbons is well made (p. 27) the bonbon will maintain its shape for many hours, though after 1 hour the texture will be too soft to pick it up with your fingers (always depending on the room temperature).

Foie bonbons with truffle

Ingredients (for 20 pieces)

- 3-1/2 oz. mix for foie bonbons (p. 27)
- 20 small pieces of truffle gelatin

Truffle gelatin

Ingredients

1 cup truffle juice
1 1/2 gelatin sheet

Method

1. *Strain the truffle juice.*
2. *Soak the gelatin in plenty of cold water.*
3. *Once it has softened, drain and heat with 2 spoonfuls of truffle juice in a saucepan over low heat.*
4. *When the gelatin has completely melted, add the rest of the truffle juice. Stir.*
5. *Pour into a flat metallic recipient to a height of 1/4 in.*
6. *Allow to gel in the refrigerator.*
7. *Once gelled, cut the gelatin into 1/4 in. strips, then square them to make dice 1/4 in. on a side.*

METHOD

1. With a spatula, fill a silicone bonbon mold with the foie mix.
2. Allow to rest in a cold storage room for 12 hours, or freeze.
3. De-mold and place a piece of truffle gelatin on top of the bonbon.
4. Store in airtight containers at 0°F (−18°C).

Note: Foie gras is a fat and can therefore easily absorb odors. For this reason, it is important to keep it well covered.

SERVING

1. Allow to thaw in a 37°F (3°C) refrigerator.
2. Do not leave at room temperature for longer than 1 hour.

Note: if the mix for foie bonbons is well made (p. 27) the bonbon will maintain its shape for many hours, though after 1 hour the texture will be too soft to pick it up with your fingers (always depending on the room temperature).

Fill the bonbon molds with a spatula.

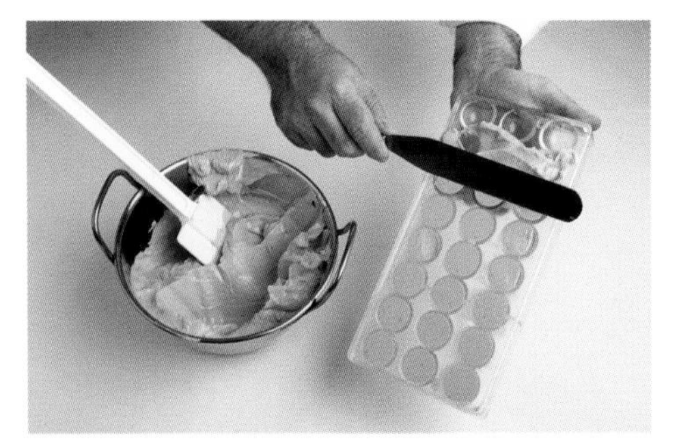

Once frozen, remove them from the mold.

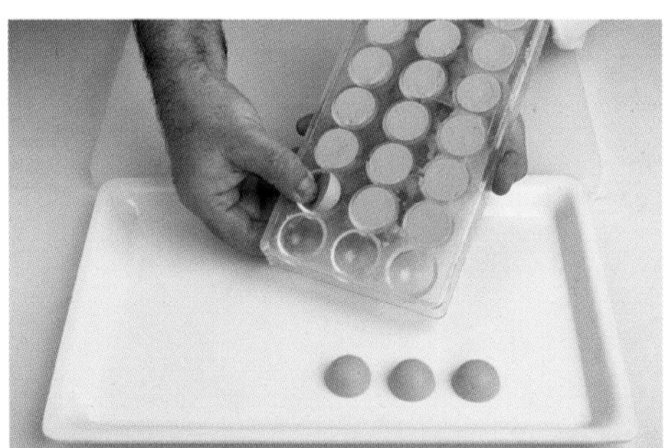

Place a truffle gelatin cube onto each bonbon.

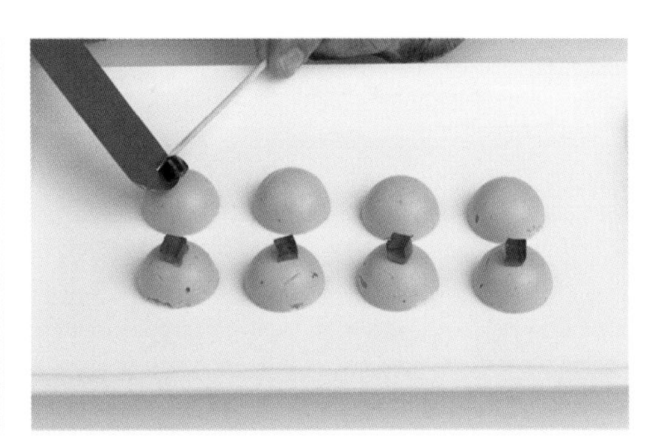

SHAPES IN TOAST

What is most innovative about these recipes is the use of par-baked bread. Previously, toast was always made with fresh or day-old bread.

The advantage of working with frozen par-baked bread is that it allows for very thin slices and makes shaping the toast very easy.

The technique is not difficult—all you need are some basic guidelines. In the following pages, I offer a series of pointers to obtain optimal results and take full advantage of this product.

As is evident in the recipes, treating par-baked bread in this way presents multiple possibilities: it can be shaped, skewered or used to wrap an ingredient into the shape of a cone or dumpling then toasted to make a delicious, hot, crunchy morsel.

Because it is so easy, this technique gives our imagination free reign to reach unforeseen limits, with results that can surprise even us.

The technique

In order to shape the toast, it is essential to slice the frozen par-baked bread very thinly.
In order to do this, it must be at a partly thawed stage—neither hard nor soft. If it is too hard (that is, 100% frozen), it can break or crack when run through the slicer; if it is too soft (100% thawed) it is impossible to slice thinly. In any case, and for the purpose of orientation, to get the optimal consistency the slicing should be done with the bread more frozen than not. We should not forget that bread has the particular quality of thawing very quickly, indeed almost immediately, for which it is not advisable to wait too long before slicing.
Once sliced, the bread must be allowed to thaw completely before it is shaped.

Let us look at the process step by step:

1. Choose the type of bread based on the shape you want to give it (see Note).
2. Thaw to a point that allows for choosing the thickness of the slice without it breaking.
3. Cut with the slicer.
4. Allow to thaw completely without drying out.
5. Shape with your hand, with the help of a mould, simply crinkle it or stick it to a bamboo skewer by pressing with your fingers.
6. Place in the oven at 300ºF (150ºC) until golden brown.
7. I recommend storing it in a closed or thermosealed container (the latter is best but only permits opening once), keeping it away from moisture.

Note: types of bread used for the recipes in this chapter:
For the cone we have used a very small round rolls because it has crust around the entire edge. When toasted, the crust becomes more solid and resistant than the inside and protects this delicate toast from possible cracks.
For the crinkled toast we have opted for one of the largest-sized par-baked breads available: "gallego" bread (country bread from the Spanish region of Galicia).
For the rest of the recipes we have played with individual ciabattas or baguettes.
In reality, any par-baked bread will allow all types of shapes, depending on the slice and our ability and imagination.

Various types of par-baked bread.

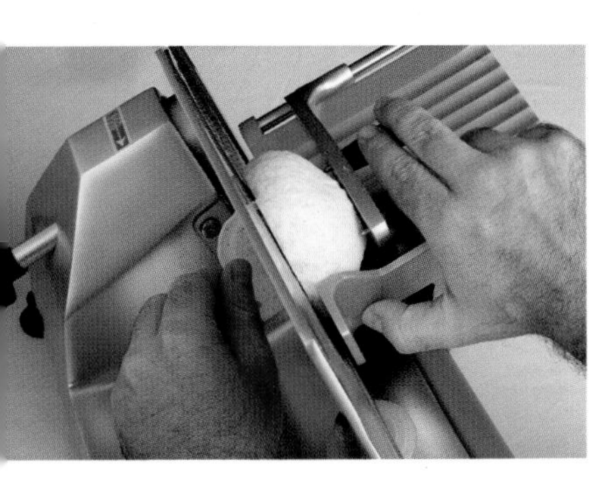

Machine slicing.

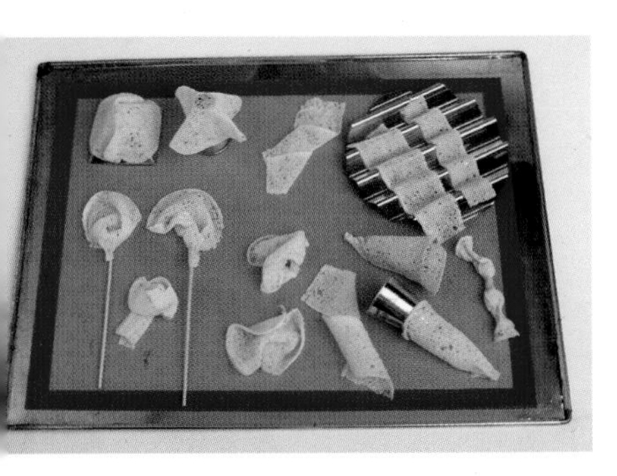

A variety of shapes: lollypops, crinkles, or molded shapes.

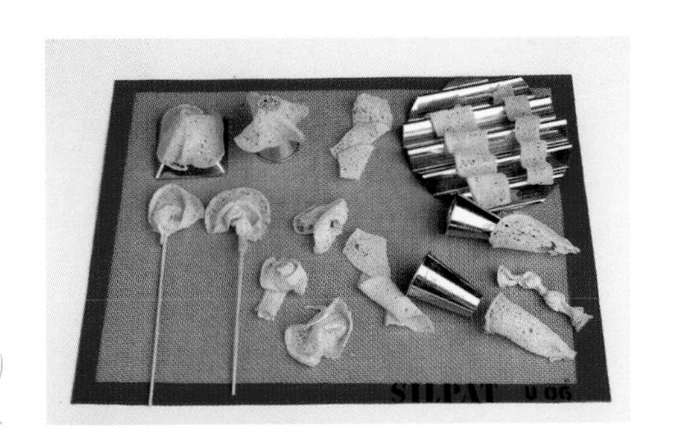

After toasting at 300°F (150°C) on a silicone sheet.

Removed from molds and ready for use.

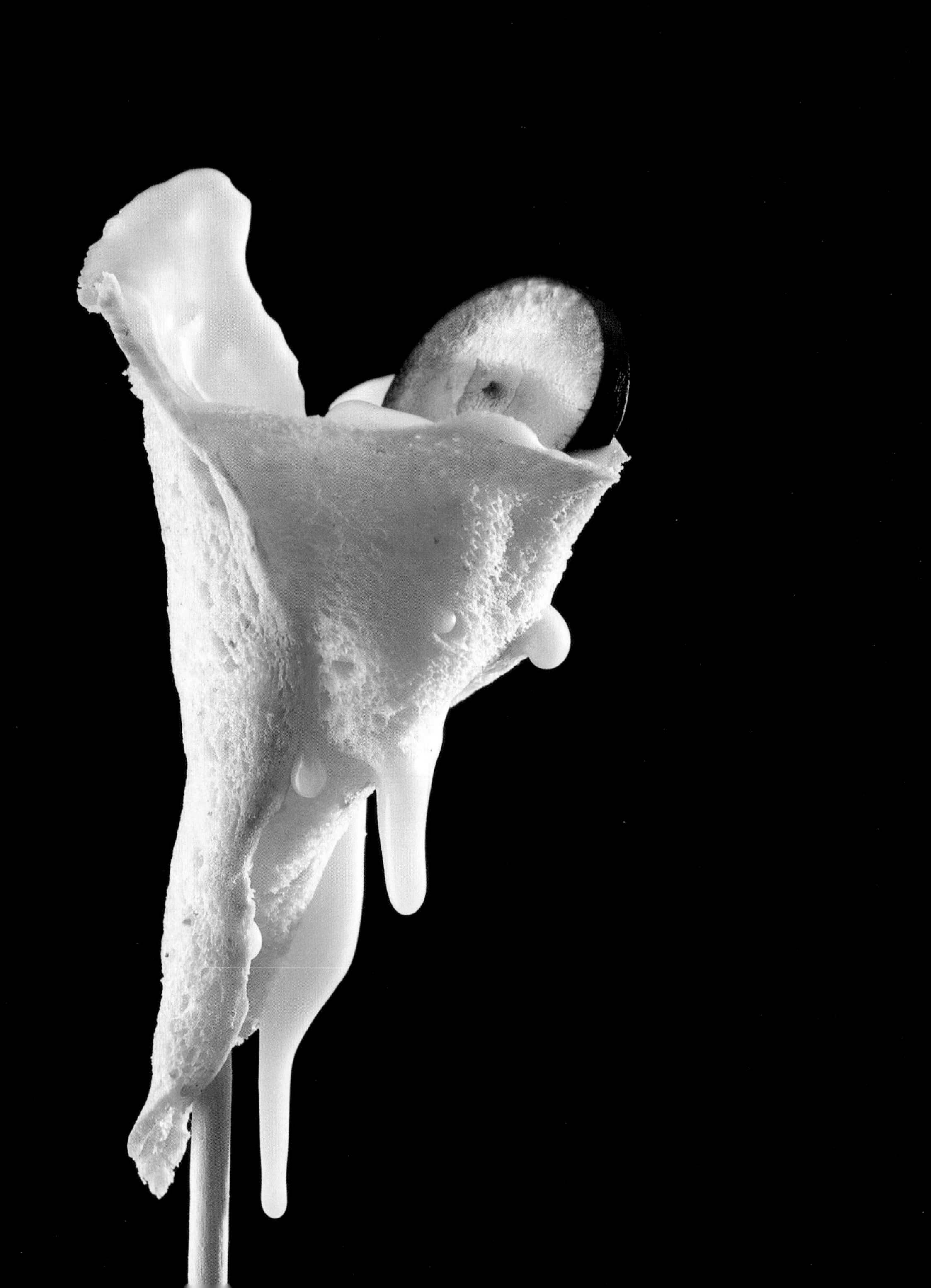

Creamy cheese and grape cone

Ingredients (for 10 pieces)

- 10 cone-shaped pieces of toast (p. 52)
- 8 oz. Torta de la Serena* cheese (soft)
- 2 grapes

Method

1. With a pastry bag, pipe 3/4 oz. of cheese into the cone.
2. Cut the grapes into 10 thin slices and place one slice per cone on top of the cheese.

Serving

1. This piece needs some support, since it must remain vertical. And it must be assembled just before serving. For this reason, I recommend having the cones shaped and ready, the cheese in the pastry bag and the grapes sliced so they can be assembled as needed. The life of these pieces will depend on the creaminess of the cheese and the room temperature.
   A practical solution would be to use a more solid cheese, though Torta de la Serena makes for a truly special mouthful.

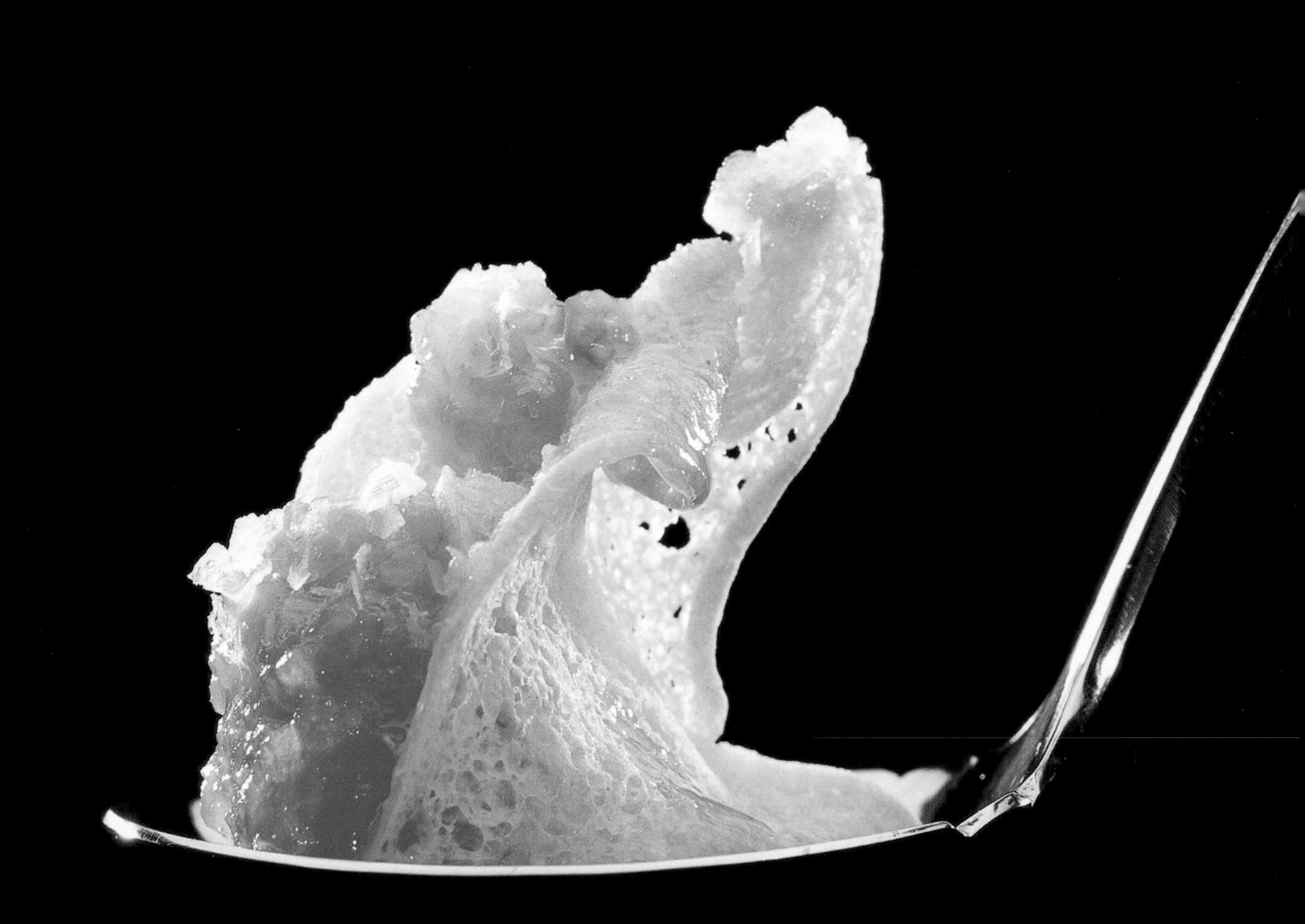

"Pan con tomate" toast

Ingredients (for 10 pieces)

- 10 crinkled pieces of toast (p. 52)
- 2 oz. sifted tomato (p. 197)
- virgin olive oil
- Maldon sea salt

Method

1. Place the toast into your chosen recipient.
2. Using a small spoon, place the sifted tomato onto the toast.
3. Top with a few salt crystals.
4. Drizzle with olive oil.
5. Serve immediately.

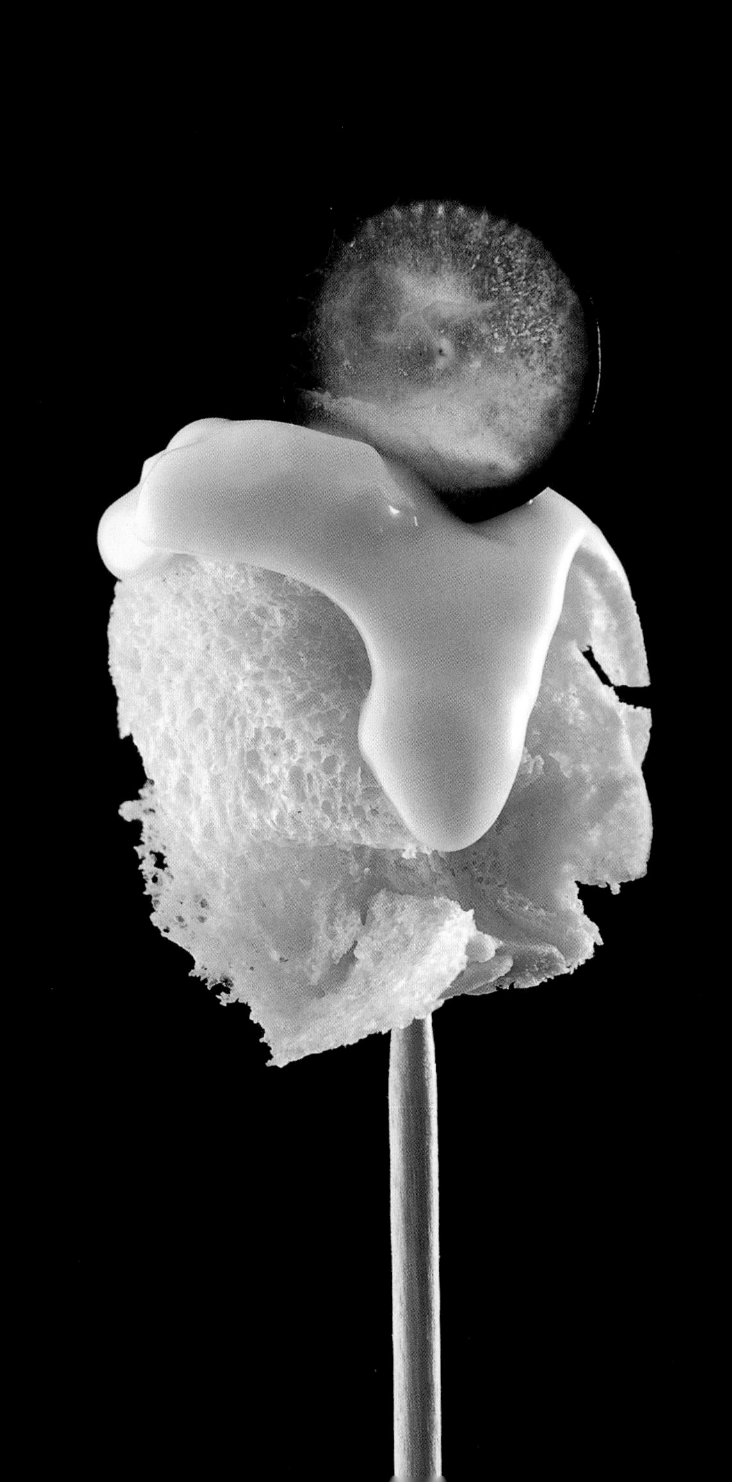

Mini toast with creamy cheese and grape

Ingredients (for 10 pieces)

- 10 crinkled toast or lollypop toast pieces (p. 52)
- 8 oz. Torta de la Serena* cheese (soft)
- 2 grapes

Method

1. With a pastry bag, pipe 1/2-3/4 oz. of cheese onto the toast.
2. Cut the grapes into 10 thin slices and place one slice per toast on top of the cheese.

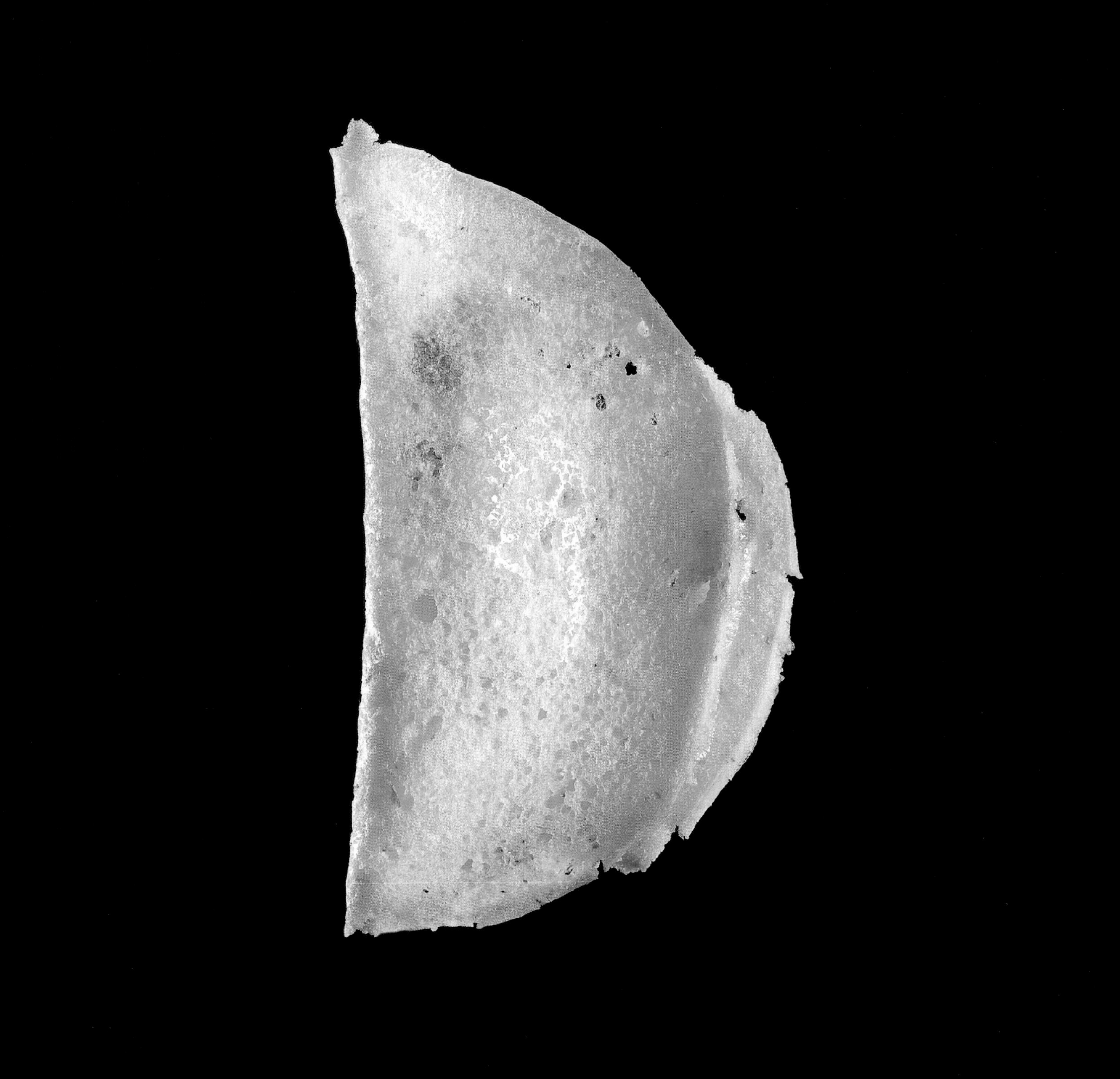

GORGONZOLA DUMPLING

INGREDIENTS (FOR 10 PIECES)

- 1 small roll, par-baked and frozen
- 1/2 cup simple syrup (p. 204)
- 5-1/2 oz. Gorgonzola cheese

METHOD

1. Thinly slice the roll (follow the instructions in the technique section, p. 52).
2. Allow the bread slices to dry slightly so that they do not absorb too much syrup.
3. Glaze them with the (cold) syrup, place them onto a silicone sheet and bake in the oven at 300°F (150°C) until golden brown.
4. Remove them from the oven and quickly place a 1/2 oz. rectangle of Gorgonzola in each. Fold them over, giving them a half-moon or dumpling shape.
5. Allow to cool.

Note: this dumpling is very crunchy and also sweet, which makes it an ideal contrast for the Gorgonzola. Remember that, over time, the bread absorbs the moisture of the cheese and loses its crunch where the two are in contact. Rather than filling the toast, another possibility is to simply (once cold) drizzle it with virgin olive oil and salt: this produces a similar flavor to that of a slice of bread with olive oil and sugar (thanks to the sweetness of the toast), but with an extremely crunchy texture.*
(* bread with olive oil and sugar was a typical snack for Spanish children in more difficult times.)

Glaze the lightly dried bread with the syrup.

Bake on a silicone sheet. Once out of the oven, fill with the Gorgonzola and shape immediately.

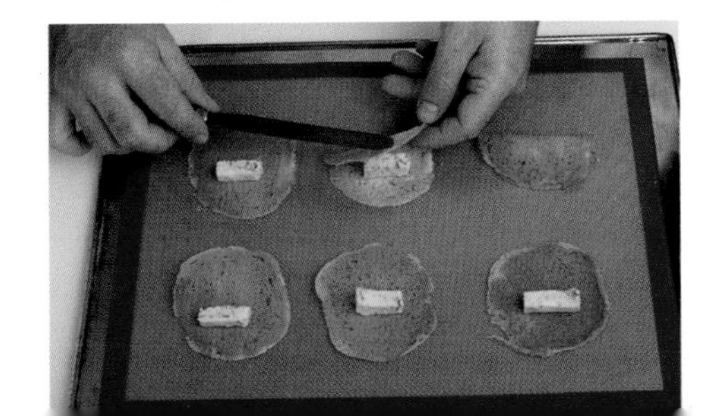

TARTARS

Legend has it that the Tartar warriors had the habit of placing a piece of raw meat between the saddle and the horse's back. After hours of riding, the meat would become similar to a type of mincemeat. Then, with the peculiar flavour given by the heat and sweat of the animal or seasoned with whatever they had, it was converted into something like what is known today as steak tartar.

Nowadays the name "tartar" is given to any dish made up of a raw ingredient, chopped and seasoned with various complementary ingredients, whether they be liquids or finely chopped solids.

Perhaps the so-called "purists", who must exist although I personally do not know any, will yell in protest when they see what this book has called "tartars".

The four "tartars" I present here do not incorporate one element that is boiled, roasted, fried, or subjected to any kind of heat treatment (except the toast and Forum reduction). They are cured (sausage, roe and parmesan) or cooked by vinegar (pickled). So I have taken the liberty of applying a gastronomic term to something that in reality only corresponds by a similarity in form, but is not too far off.

There is no particular technique for this preparation, save for some cutting detail described in the course of the recipes. The fundamental point here is knowing how to eat it. The presentation, which combines numerous little elements into a small dish, requires the use of a spoon to pick up the most ingredients possible and eat them in one bite, and then repeat this action a few times. The simultaneous tasting of the distinct ingredients is what makes this aperitif unique, since by themselves they are well-known flavours.

Fruit and vegetable tartar with caviar

Ingredients (for 10 servings)

- 1 oz. red pepper
- 1 oz. cauliflower
- 1 oz. fresh green beans
- 1 oz. mango
- 1 oz. yellow pitahaya
- 1 oz. papaya
- 1 oz. pineapple
- 1 oz. *nashi hosui* (Asian pear)

Note: all very finely diced (dice should be maximum 1/8 in. on a side)

- 3-1/2 oz. herring caviar
- 1/2 cup virgin olive oil
- 2 tbsp. soy and wine reduction (p. 193)

Assembly

1. Group the fruit and vegetables into small mounds or narrow strips equal in size and volume.
2. Top with a little caviar and dress with olive oil.
3. Drizzle with the soy and wine reduction.

Note: this can be done with the fruits and vegetables of choice, but I recommend playing with the most distinct textures, colors and flavors possible to obtain contrast. There is no need for salt—the caviar provides it, among other things.

Cured sausage and tomato tartar

Ingredients (for 10 servings)

- 1-1/2 oz. toasted croutons, 1/4 in. on a side.
- 7 oz. *fuet* from Vic
- 5-1/2 oz. sifted tomato (p. 197)
- Maldon sea salt
- virgin olive oil
- freshly ground black pepper

Note: the fuet *is a thin, cured sausage traditionally made in Vic (province of Barcelona, Spain)*

Method

1. Remove the skin from the *fuet*.
2. Cut lengthwise into strips about 1/4 in. wide.
3. Cut these strips along the width to make 1/4 in. x 1/4 in. dice.

Assembly

1. Spoon a small mound of drained tomato into the centre of the chosen dish.
2. Spread the fuet and bread dice over the tomato.
3. Sparingly top with grains of salt.
4. Give it a few turns of the peppermill and dress generously with virgin olive oil.

Note: obviously, the fuet *can be substituted for other cured meats, and the same recipe can also be done with the cheese of choice.*

Roe and pickle tartar

Ingredients (for 10 servings)

- 2 oz. pickled carrots
- 2 oz. pickled cauliflower
- 2 oz. pickled gherkins
- 1 oz. raw green beans
- 1-1/2 oz. toasted croutons

Note: all very finely diced (dice should be max. 1/4 in. on a side)

- 7 oz. cured tuna or hake roe
- extra virgin olive oil
- 5-1/2 oz. tomato purée

Method

1. Dice the roe to the same size as the croutons.
2. Mix all of the pickled vegetables together and add the oil. Stir.
3. Spoon the mixture of pickled vegetable and oil into the center of the chosen dish.
4. Place the roe dice onto the vegetables and top with the croutons.
5. Spoon small mounds of tomato sparingly onto the dish and, lastly, sprinkle with the very finely diced raw green beans.

Note: this tartar can be prepared with diced raw fish (tuna, salmon, etc.) and a little soy sauce and sesame oil instead of olive oil. Or with smoked fish, salted anchovies, etc., substituting or adding elements as desired.

Arugula and Parmesan tartar

Ingredients (for 10 servings)

- 2 oz. arugula
- 3-1/2 oz. Parmesan cheese
- 10 shaped pieces of toast (to taste) (p. 52)
- 3-1/2 oz. balsamic vinegar reduction (p. 192)
- pepper
- virgin olive oil

Method

1. Use a knife to cut thin strips of arugula.
2. Finely grate the Parmesan with an extra-fine grater.
3. Mix the arugula and Parmesan into a ball shape.

Assembly

1. Place the arugula and Parmesan ball into the centre of the chosen dish.
2. Place a piece of shaped toast to one side of the ball.
3. Drizzle with virgin olive oil.
4. Pour in a generous drop of balsamic vinegar reduction.
5. Place a small mound of freshly ground pepper to the side.

Note: finely chopped tomato can be added to this tartar, with the arugula substituted for basil.

Glasses

I do not think that the person who designed the small glasses that appear in our restaurants and gala catering trays filled with solid food imagined at the time that they would have this function.

The Amaro glass has been used to serve all types of appetizers and cocktails and has virtually become a classic for this end. It is one of the most popular for its design—a curved base that facilitates extracting the last bit of food with a small spoon. Its thin conical shape allows one to clearly see what is inside and accommodates appetizers with very delicate or liquid textures. I have used this glass to serve a liquid hors d'oeuvre that is very fresh and uniquely colored.

The Borrell liquor glass is shorter, more rounded and open-mouthed than the former. This glass used to be typical for serving muscatel and dessert wines. It also has ideal qualities for this application, and it is very stable.

Lastly, the Vinum Spirits liquor glasses made by prestigious Riedel have been used. It is like a formal gala dress—uncomfortable, delicate and expensive—though from my point of view it is worth suffering these inconveniences to present a product with a simple but very elegant design.

The diffused glasses that I present in this chapter are inspired by the properties of Micri, a revolutionary product created by Miguel Sánchez Romera, chef and owner of the L'Esguard restaurant in Llavaneras (Barcelona, Spain) and distributed by specialized providers. Micri is a completely colorless, tasteless and odorless vegetable base which acts as a texturizer, de-coagulant, stabilizer, anti-crystallizer and emulsifier in various preparations in savory cooking and patisserie, in which it intensifies aromas without stripping ingredients of their nature. And it has the additional advantage of being fat-free.

When applied to the preparation of diffused glasses, Micri allows the mixture of yogurt with fruits and vegetables to "sustain itself". The resulting consistency permits us to play with a myriad of flavors and colors all converted to the same texture and prevents them from mixing together when added in a specific order to a glass. Though if preferred, they can be subtly mixed together to diffuse the colors and create very aesthetic designs and chromatic plays. This combination of flavors and textures at very cold temperature (without freezing) is exquisite, very refreshing and pleasing to the palate.

The technique: diffused glasses

In preparing these chilled glasses it is essential to choose the fruits and vegetables carefully: they will mix in one's mouth in a variety of ways depending on how the glass is filled and how each distinct preparation is taken with the spoon. This means that we will taste one, two, three or more flavors, separately or combined.
Diffused glasses can be prepared with any desired fruits and vegetables by following the steps below:

1. Blanch the fruits and vegetables in boiling water and chill in ice water.
2. Liquefy them, or, if impossible, purée and strain them as finely as possible (each fruit and vegetable separately).
3. To each juice obtained, add a maximum of 20% Micri.

Note: for these preparations, the Micri must always be used at ribbon stage: blend it with a hand-held blender and a little water until it attains a more fluid texture that facilitates mixing.

4. Adjust quantities of salt, sugar and lemon juice if necessary to balance flavors.
5. Mix with Greek-style plain yogurt and purée in a blender, with a hand-held mixer or in a Thermomix. The texture of the yogurt will break, yielding a softer, more diffused coloring.
6. Set aside each mixture separately in squeeze dispensers (I recommend labeling each dispenser with the name of the flavor).
7. Allow to rest about 4 hours at 37°F (3°C).
8. Alternate pouring small amounts into the glass, combining colors and flavors to taste.
9. Always serve chilled.

Note: prepared glasses will last for hours outside or in the fridge, though I recommend always serving them chilled.

In the recipes that follow, I suggest a series of flavor combinations that I consider successful and delightful. However, they are nothing more than that, suggestions; from there, the possibilities are endless. It is not possible, nor do I believe useful, to specify the exact quantities of the various yogurts used to fill a glass; this depends greatly on the taste and criteria of each person as well as the glass used. Nevertheless, and as a reference, the Amaro glass, which is the one used to present these preparations, has a capacity for 2 oz. of yogurt. I recommend never adding more than about 1/2 oz. of one flavor, and combining a minimum of 3 different flavors.

Fruits and vegetables.

Blanch and chill.

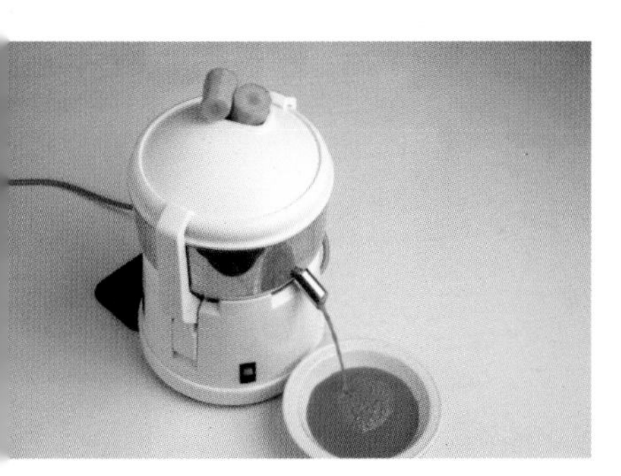

Liquefy.

Liquefied fruits and vegetables.

Emulsify juice, Micri and yogurt with the blender.

Fruit and Vegetable Glass Nº 1

Ingredients

- Yogurt with melon Micri
- Yogurt with beet Micri
- Yogurt with red pepper Micri
- Yogurt with blood orange Micri
- Yogurt with asparagus Micri

Assembly

(see diffused glass technique, p. 74).

1. Pour a large base of yogurt with melon Micri.
2. Touching the point of the dispensing cup to the inside of the glass, pour a small amount of the yogurt with beet Micri.
3. Fill the rest of the glass with the other yogurt with Micri flavors.

Fruit and vegetable glass Nº 2

Ingredients

- Yogurt with melon Micri
- Yogurt with red pepper Micri
- Yogurt with green pepper Micri
- Yogurt with beet Micri
- Yogurt with blood orange Micri
- Passion fruit Micri (p. 74)

Assembly

(see diffused glass technique, p. 74).

1. Pour a small base of yogurt with melon, red pepper, and green pepper Micri and passion fruit Micri.
2. Top with a thick layer of yogurt with melon and beet Micri.
3. Finish with small quantities of yogurt with blood orange and green pepper Micri and drizzle with passion fruit Micri.

Fruit and vegetable glass Nº 3

Ingredients

- Yogurt with melon Micri
- Yogurt with beet Micri
- Yogurt with red pepper Micri
- Yogurt with blood orange Micri
- Yogurt with asparagus Micri
- Yogurt with carrot Micri
- Passion fruit Micri (p. 74)

Assembly

(see diffused glass technique, p. 74).

1. Pour a base of yogurt with beet Micri.
2. Cover with a layer of melon yogurt.
3. Pour in small spots of all of the yogurts with Micri and spots of passion fruit Micri.
4. Top with melon and finish with small amounts of yogurt with asparagus, blood orange and red pepper Micri.

Fruit and vegetable glass Nº 4

Ingredients

- Yogurt with melon Micri
- Yogurt with beet Micri
- Yogurt with blood orange Micri
- Yogurt with carrot Micri
- Passion fruit Micri (p. 74)

Assembly

(see diffused glass technique, p. 74).

1. Begin filling with small amounts of each yogurt with Micri in random order, sporadically inserting a few drops of passion fruit Micri for a touch of acidity.
2. Follow with more generous quantities of beet and blood orange yogurt. Once again, drizzle in a few drops of passion fruit.
3. Before finishing the glass, add some yogurt with melon Micri to intensify the contrast of flavors and colors.
4. Finish with the same flavors that started the glass.

Marine foie with salmon roe

Ingredients (for 20 servings)

- 2/3 lbs. marine foie
- 3-1/2 oz. salmon roe
- 10 pieces of shaped toast (p. 52)
- dill sprigs (optional)

Marine foie

Ingredients

17-1/2 oz. canned smoked cod liver
1 tsp. Modena balsamic vinegar

Method

1. *Open the cod liver cans and drain. Save the oil in a bowl.*
2. *Place the cod livers in the Thermomix together with the balsamic vinegar.*
3. *Blend the livers to make a smooth cream and emulsify with their oil by pouring it in very slowly and continuously.*

Note: use only the amount of oil necessary to obtain the desired texture.
If enough of the cod liver does not reach the Thermomix blades, it is difficult to get a good emulsion.
This marine foie can be an excellent spread: it is delicious on a piece of toast with an anchovy on top. It is also perfect for fish dishes, in the manner of *maître d'hôtel* butter for example.

Assembly

1. Spoon the marine foie into a pastry bag at a temperature between 37°F (3°C) and 41°F and (5°C).
2. Fill the glass with about 1 oz.
3. Place a small spoonful of salmon roe in the center.
4. Insert a shaped piece of toast and garnish with fresh dill.

Cauliflower with Caviar and Mango

Ingredients (for 10 servings)

- 2/3 lbs. cauliflower purée
- 7 oz. caviar
- 7 oz. g mango, diced (maximum 1/8 in. on a side)

Cauliflower purée

Ingredients

1 cauliflower
2 qt. milk
3 oz. butter
salt

Method

1. *Clean, chop and wash the cauliflower.*
2. *Bring the milk to a boil and add the cauliflower.*
3. *Once cooked, drain, keeping the milk. Place the cauliflower with the butter into the Thermomix. Salt to taste.*
4. *Purée at high speed with heat and add part of the milk if necessary. Allow to cool.*

Assembly

1. Gently mix the cauliflower purée with the caviar and mango (set aside a bit of caviar and mango to finish the glass).
2. Fill a glass to the top using a pastry bag, starting with the bag at the bottom to avoid air pockets.
3. Use a spatula to even the top and leave the purée up to the brim.
4. Garnish with a bit of caviar and mango dice.

Truffle yogurt

Ingredients (for 10 cupfuls)

- 2 Greek yogurt servings
- 1/4 cup Piamonte white truffle *(Tuber magnatum)* oil
- 1/2 cup truffle *(Tuber melanosporum)* juice
- 1 large (about 1 oz.) truffle *(Tuber melanosporum)*
- 1 small potato
- 1/2 cup base syrup (p. 204)
- 1/2 gelatin sheet

Method

1. Cut the peeled potato into 20 dice 1/4 in. on a side and boil for a few minutes in the syrup.
2. Very finely grate the entire truffle and spread out the resulting powder so that it dries a bit. Set aside.
3. Empty the Greek yogurt into a stainless steel bowl and emulsify with an egg beater, slowly and continuously pouring in the white truffle oil.
4. Melt the pre-soaked gelatin sheet with a bit of truffle juice and add it to the rest of the juice. Stir and strain.
5. Coat the potato dice with half of the truffle powder.

Assembly

1. Pour a 3/8 in. layer of gelled truffle juice into the bottom of the glass and dust with a pinch of truffle powder. Allow to set at 37°F (3°C).
2. Cover this gelatin with a 5/8 in. layer of Greek yogurt emulsified with white truffle oil.
3. Place two candied truffle-covered potato dice on top of the yogurt.
4. Serve chilled.

Bamboo skewers

Bamboo skewers have long been and continue to be the most commonly used tool for picking up various ingredients and bringing them all to one's mouth in a comfortable, clean way without the need for utensils.
This simple tool quickly and easily solves some of the dilemmas encountered by a chef when the time comes to present an hors d'oeuvre. And with excellent results–it doesn't require a base of any kind, allows one to avoid touching the food with one's fingers and keeps the skewered elements from "dancing" on the plate.
This is not by any means a new concept, especially in Spain, where appetizers (olives, cockles, cheese cubes, etc.) have always been served with toothpicks. Many establishments serve Spanish Omelet squares already pierced with toothpicks. Not to mention the well-known martini olive: thanks to the toothpick, the consumer avoids having to put his/her fingers into the glass to fish out the olive after finishing the drink. "Banderillas" (a typical Spanish appetizer), some as famous as "gildas" (composed of anchovy, Basque chili pepper and olive), take the idea further and present various elements already skewered onto one toothpick.
Like the common toothpick, the 5 in., 6 in., 7 in. and up to 9 in. bamboo skewer has been quite common for years. And even with the wide selection of small containers available in the market for this purpose, it continues to be a great solution. Moreover, it is disposable and cheap: can one ask for more from an extremely minimalist, simple, clean piece of design?

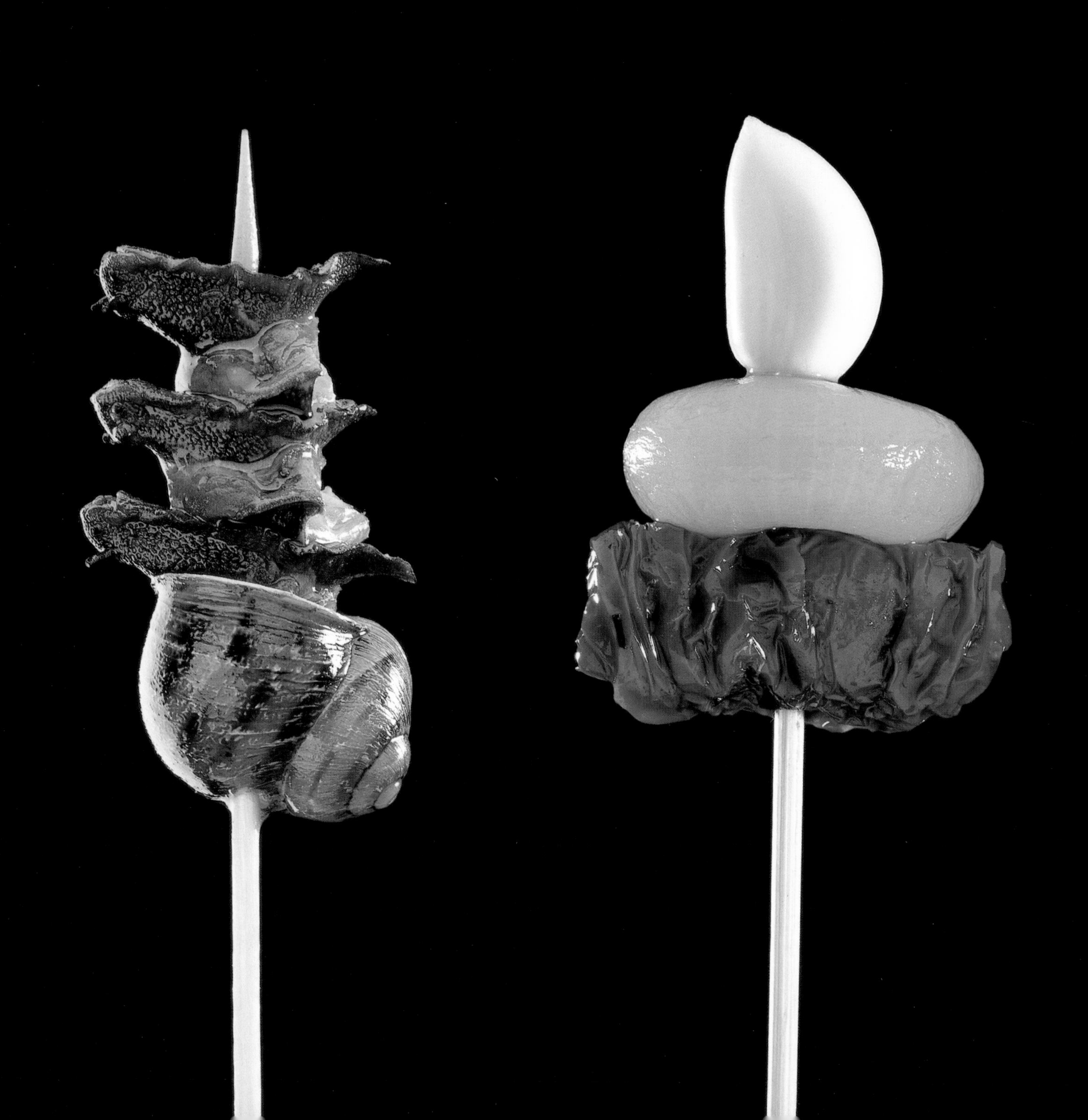

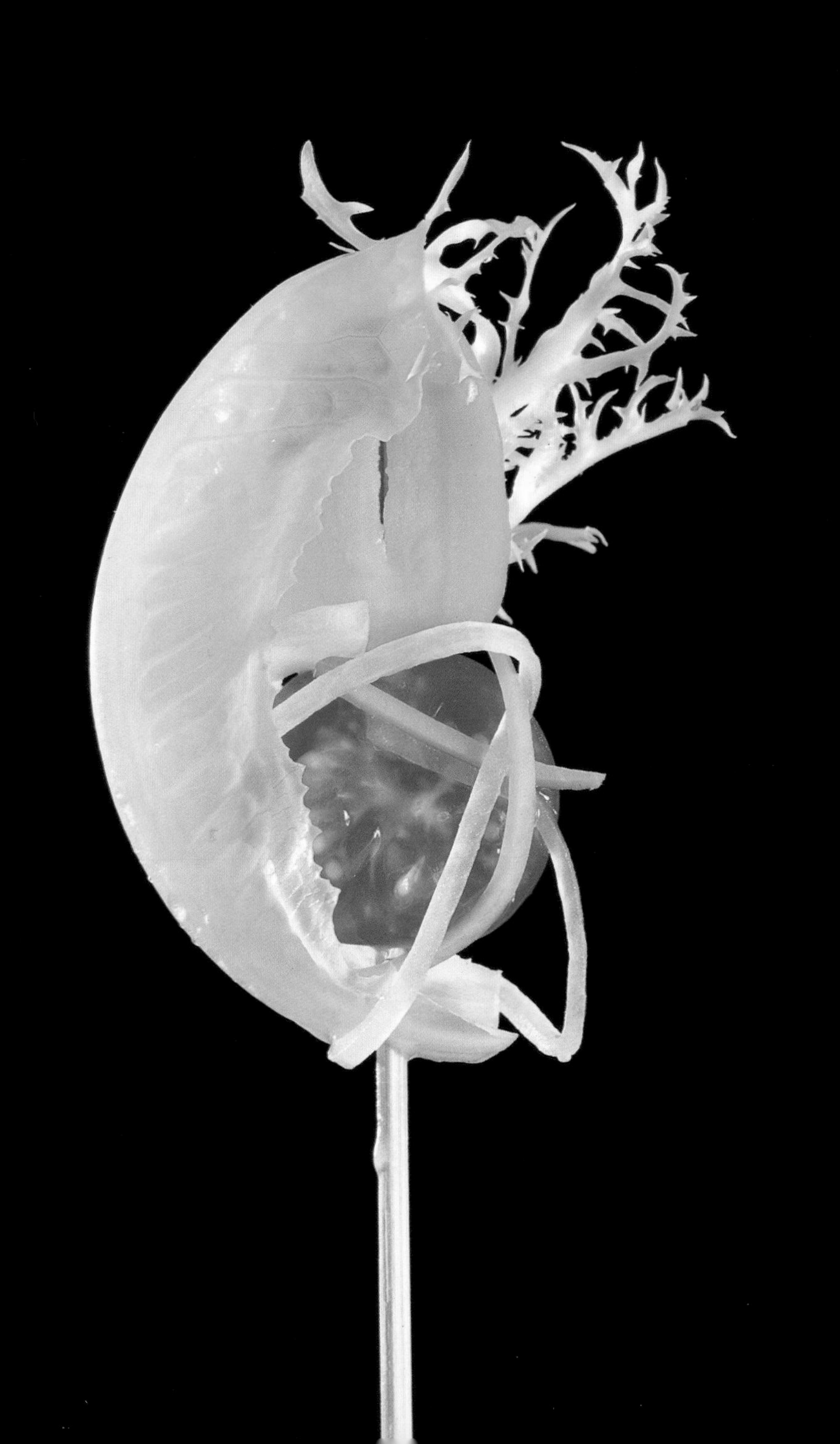

Green salad skewer

INGREDIENTS

- Romaine lettuce
- Cherry tomato
- Carrot
- Spring onion
- Curly endive
- Gordal* olive

METHOD

1. Separate the outer leaves from the lettuce for other use and keep the ones in the heart, the smallest and lightest in color. Crisp them in ice water.
2. Do the same with the curly endive.
3. Peal and cut the carrot lengthwise into 1/16 in. slices using the slicer. Then cut these into the finest possible strips. Chill in salted ice water.
4. Cut the spring onion into fine strips as with the carrot, and place them also in salted ice water.
5. Slice the olive into 4-5 round pieces with a knife.

ASSEMBLY

1. Skewer the lettuce leaf, half a cherry tomato and wrap the carrot and onion strips.
2. Place a piece of gordal olive touching the cherry tomato and a small curly endive leaf between the two.
3. I recommend dressing with oil, vinegar and salt.

Note: this skewer can be served as an appetizer as well as for a cocktail party—its role is to offer something fresh for your mouth after having tried fattier items like fried ones, cured meats, rice dishes, fondues, etc. It has a dual function: its size allows all of the flavors of a green salad to be eaten in one bite, and furthermore it is not filling.

Canned vegetable skewer

Ingredients

- Sun-dried tomato in oil
- Baby onions in balsamic vinegar
- Garlic in white vinegar
- Black olive tapenade (optional)
  (black olive paste or crushed black olives)

Assembly

1. Roll up the tomato width-wise and skewer.
2. Skewer the baby onion on top.
3. Finish with the garlic pierced vertically, making sure that the end coincides with the end of the skewer without it piercing through.
4. Serve as is or coat lightly with the tapenade.

ESCARGOTS CONFIT SKEWER

INGREDIENTS

- 2-3/16 lbs. escargots, blanched once
- stewing oil (p. 204)

METHOD

1. Place the blanched escargots in a clay pot or saucepan and cover them in stewing oil.
2. Place the pot over low heat and do not let the oil heat more than just a slow attempt at boiling. Simmer for about 1 hour.
3. Remove from heat and keep the escargot in the oil until serving.

Note: here the escargots are used for a skewer. However, this technique was developed for finishing them in a clay pot, lightly drained of oil with a pinch of flour, salt and pepper. It is all lightly stirred to end up with magnificent escargots, as Mr. Norton from "La Bolera" restaurant in Canyet (Badalona, Spain) showed me.

ASSEMBLY

1. Remove the escargot from their shells with a burin and keep the nicest shells (choose one out of every 3 snails).
2. Discard the inedible parts.
3. Skewer the escargot shell, the hole previously made with the diameter of the skewer.
4. Then skewer the three shelled escargots. Coat with their oil and serve. Alternatively, they may be coated with truffle mayonnaise (p. 194).

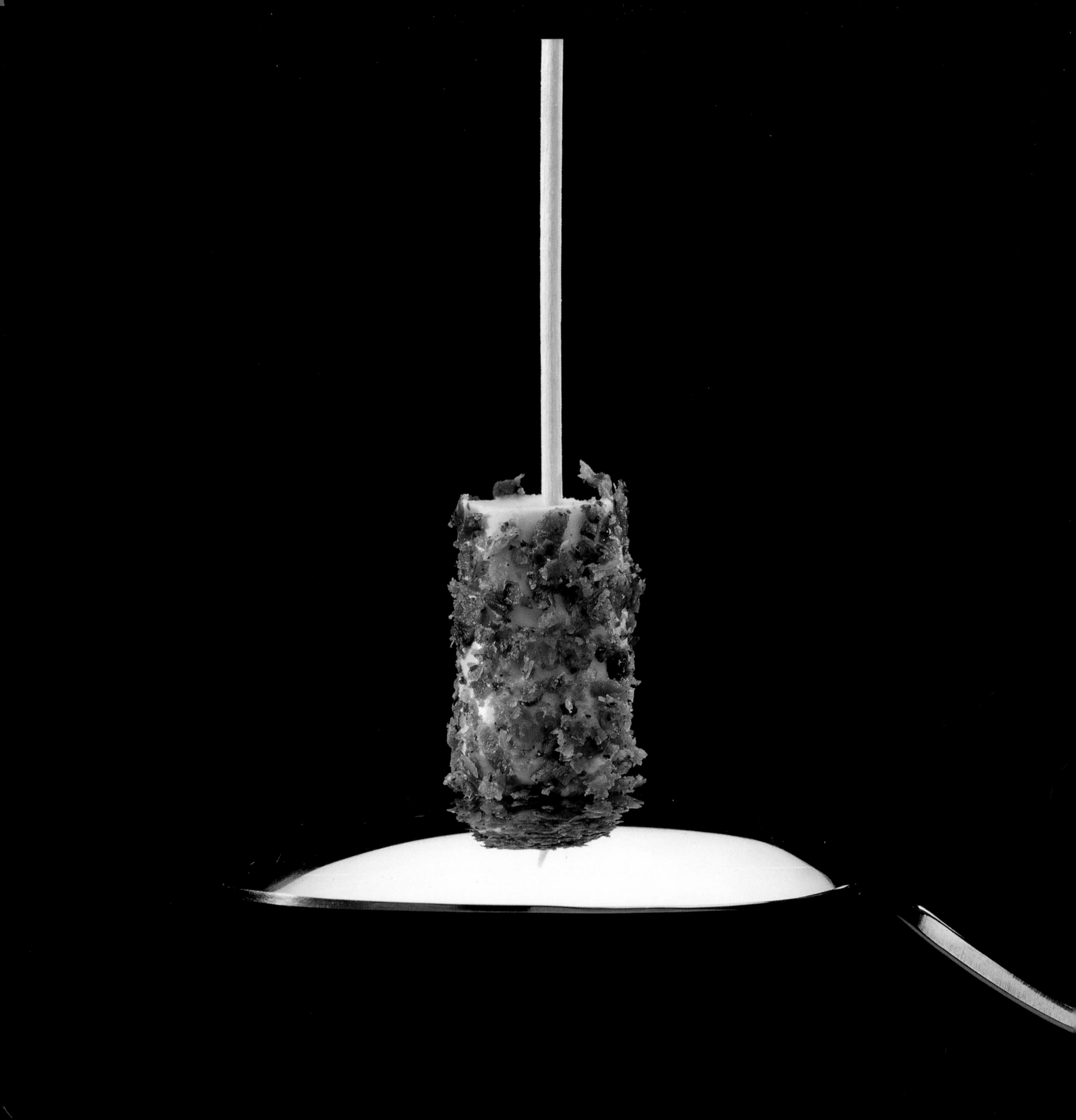

ROTISSERIE CHICKEN SKEWER

INGREDIENTS (FOR 35 PIECES)

- 17-1/2 oz. chicken roasted with apples
- 1 oz. chicken skin crocanti
- 1 oz. cream

CHICKEN ROASTED WITH APPLES

INGREDIENTS

1 chicken, about 3 lbs. in weight
1 apple
1/4 tsp. curry
1/4 tsp. black pepper
1 tsp. salt
1/2 tsp. sugar
1/2 tsp. rosemary
1/4 tsp. thyme
1/4 tsp. bay leaves
4 garlic cloves, finely chopped
1/2 lemon with peel, diced
white wine
olive oil

METHOD

1. *Remove the guts from the chicken and make sure its feathers are well plucked.*
2. *Stuff with the mixture of herbs, garlic and lemon.*
3. *Rub all of the skin with the previously mixed curry, pepper, salt and sugar.*
4. *Chop the apple.*
5. *Roast the chicken and apple in the oven or on a rotisserie for 1 hour 15 minutes, drizzling with olive oil and white wine periodically.*

CHICKEN SKIN CROCANTI

INGREDIENTS

The roast chicken skin

METHOD

1. *Lay out the skin onto a silicone sheet.*
2. *Dry with a crumpled paper towel, pressing it onto the skin.*
3. *Top with another silicone sheet and toast in the oven at 320ºF (160ºC) for about 30 minutes or until golden brown.*
4. *Remove from the oven and allow the skin to cool on a non-stick sheet.*
5. *Once cool and crispy, chop finely with a knife.*

Note: if when cool it is not crispy, place again in the oven. Some parts of the skin may still not be crispy; in this case, discard them and use only the crispy pieces.

6. *Store in an airtight container with a moisture absorber.*

Place the skin between two silicone sheets to put in the oven.

Chop very finely with a knife.

ASSEMBLY

1. Blend the chicken meat, peeled apples and cream in the Thermomix with heat until it has a very fine texture.
2. Make a PVC cylinder 5/8 in. in diameter and 1-5/8 in. high.
3. On a flat surface, arrange metallic rings and place the PVC cylinders inside them so that they touch each other and hold each other upright.
4. Use a pastry bag to fill the cylinders with the chicken purée. Insert a 5 in. bamboo skewer in the center of each cylinder, making sure they are as vertical as possible.
5. Refrigerate at 37°F (3°C) for 6 hours. Remove the PVC.
6. Spread the chicken skin crocanti onto a tray. Roll each cylinder and serve.

Separate the meat from the skin.

Purée the chicken.

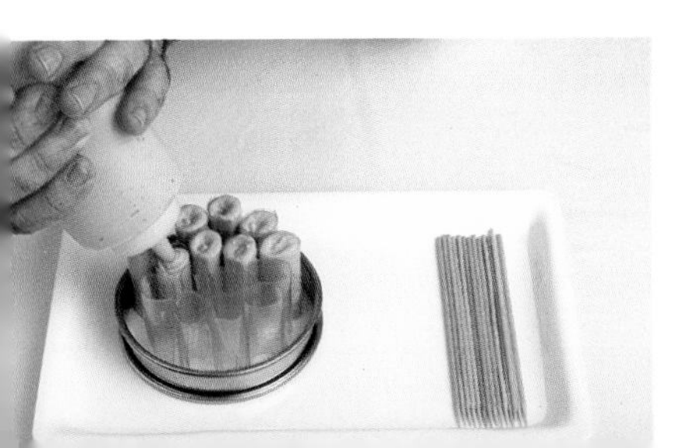

Fill the cylinders.

Insert the skewers and refrigerate.

Roll the cylinders in the chicken skin crocanti.

Fried morsels

Fry, fried, refried... These are the most common of words in our world, concepts that are part of daily life. That is why I sometimes have the impression that they are not given the importance they deserve. Even so, I find the technique of frying to be one of the most difficult. Contrary to what many might think, it is something very serious and not at all easy—it is a process that requires the utmost dexterity and attention. Its success depends on the temperature of the oils, their fusion points, the tools used and of course the ingredient fried and oil or fat used, not to mention the precise moment in which the elements must be removed and dried while hot.

A small fish, well breaded, fried in clean oil at the right temperature for the right amount of time and allowed to drain in a strainer or on absorbent paper becomes something very representative of Spanish cuisine called "pescaíto frito". Something perhaps not very sophisticated, but it can be tricky and requires a lot more technique than it might seem. Otherwise, why is fish not fried better anywhere other than Andalusia or Japan? Why does no one know how to do it as well as Andalusian or Japanese fry-cooks?

In all of the preparations in this chapter, the same medium and the same frying tool have been used: olive oil and a frying pan. What does vary, obviously, is the food that is fried and the composition of the coating (sesame, flour, dehydrated vegetables, or simply nothing). So the only thing I have done is to substitute in some cases the bread crumbs and flour with other ingredients that can "handle" frying. That is why I do not think we can address a particular technique with respect to these recipes.

In any case, in the methods for preparation I describe certain tricks for obtaining optimal results. For example, to make the monkfish breaded with vegetables (here the word "breaded", which comes from bread, is purely analogical), they must be dehydrated or lightly dried. The monkfish must also be previously sautéed, boiled or poached so that it can later be fried in a shorter amount of time. Only in this way are the vegetables not burnt and the inside of the morsel at the desired cooking point.

Cod, orange and sesame croquette

Ingredients (for 25 pieces of about 1 oz. each)

- 21 oz. béchamel for croquettes (p. 198)
- 5-1/2 oz. de-salted cod (left quite salty)
- 1 tsp. orange dust (p. 191)
- olive oil
- flour
- sesame seeds

Method

1. Put the cod in a pot with a little water and a few drops of oil over low heat. When it reaches a boil, leave for a few seconds then turn off the heat, cover and allow to cool.
2. Mix the béchamel with the cod and all of its juice, add the orange dust and emulsify in the blender.
3. Fill a petits fours-shaped silicone mold with the béchamel emulsified with the cod and orange. Freeze for 12 hours.
4. Remove from the mold, coat in flour, then with egg and roll in the sesame seeds.
5. Fry as you would any other croquette.

Note: another option for the batter is to mix sesame seeds and bread crumbs in equal parts—it yields excellent results.

Fill silicone molds and freeze. Then remove.

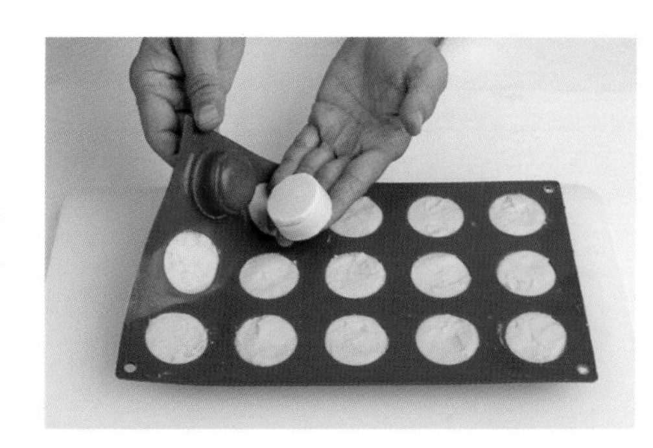

Calamari tentacles and tripe

Ingredients (for 10 pieces)

- 10 fresh un-cleaned squid, about 8 in. in length
- 2 oz. flour for frying
- olive oil (enough to fry well in the pan)
- salt

Method

1. Carefully separate the squid tentacles from the mantle, making sure not to separate the entrails from the tentacles.
2. Discard only the small sack with liquid excrement—most importantly, keep the ink and iodine sacks (black and light brown, respectively)—these are what will give this dish its special flavor.

Note: these parts of the squid are very prized in authentic seaside cuisine in taverns, cantinas, fishermen's restaurants, and by the fishermen themselves. They are used to give flavor to suquets* *(a seafood stew typical of Northeastern Spain) and rice dishes. It is true that in many places there is no custom of using these parts of the squid. In any case, one must be careful with the squid's origin and quality.*

3. Salt, coat in flour and fry.

Note: to achieve the result in the photograph, those who would like to and have the time may use frying paste (p. 205). If not, the flour for frying I suggest in this recipe yields excellent results and is much less laborious.

4. Drain on absorbent paper. Serve.

Note: the absorbent paper in this case has only relative importance, since the absorption time needs to be short. One must be careful, however—some absorbent papers on the market give off flavors and aromas to food very easily.

Remove the tentacles with the entrails without separating them. Discard the excrement sack and keep the others.

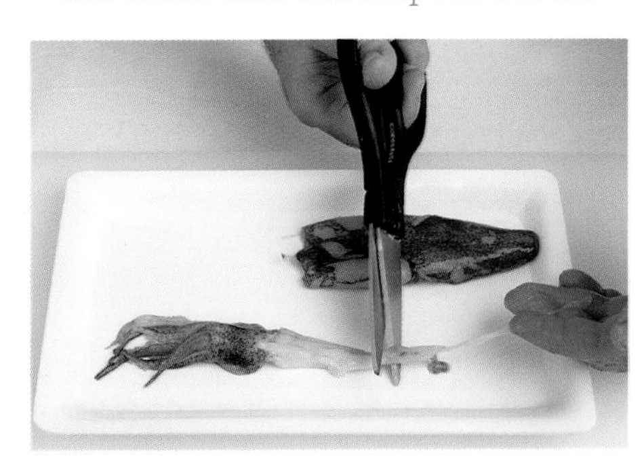

Potatoes with chorizo

Ingredients (for 20 pieces)

- 1 large Monalisa potato
- 7 oz. tender Spanish *chorizo* (not cured)

Method

1. Peel, wash and dry the potato.
2. Use a slicer to cut the potato into extremely thin slices, then spread them over paper and add salt.
3. Cut the chorizo into 1-5/8 in. x 3/8 in. rectangles (approximate thickness: 1/4 in.).
4. Place the rectangles onto the potatoes and roll them up. Lightly salt once again.
5. Fry under medium heat until lightly golden, never longer.

Note: it is important to be very attentive: the potato is cut so thinly that it can fry very quickly, change in color and flavor and end up being something quite different from the original idea.

6. Drain for a few seconds on absorbent paper.

Assembly

1. Lay them in pyramid shape onto an adequate serving dish and serve as you would croquettes or a similar dish.

Thinly slice the potato. Lay out on a flat surface, top with the chorizo *rectangles and roll up.*

Monkfish "Breaded" with Vegetables

Ingredients (for 10 pieces)

- 10 monkfish cubes, 1 oz. each
- 2 oz. dehydrated vegetables for "breading"
- olive oil
- salt
- beaten eggs

Dehydrated Vegetables for "Breading"

Ingredients

Peppers
Onions
Carrots
Asparagus
Cauliflower
Fresh green beans

Drying the vegetables in a dehydrator.

Method

1. *Chop all of the vegetables as finely as possible. Using the tip of a knife, make the cleanest slices possible without crushing the ingredients.*
2. *Place in a food dehydrator for a minimum of 4 hours (they do not need to be completely dehydrated).*

Note: if you do not have an electric dehydrator, use a convection oven at low temperature and dry the previously chopped vegetables widely spread out on a silicone sheet.

ASSEMBLY

1. Sauté the monkfish pieces.
2. Dip in the egg batter.
3. "Bread" with the dehydrated vegetables.
4. Fry in olive oil so that the vegetables do not brown too much (they should not lose their original color).

Note: it is important to make sure the monkfish is perfectly cooked and the vegetables retain their original color. This is why the monkfish pieces are first sautéed. This way, once they are "breaded" we can lightly fry them and achieve optimal results.

SERVING

In reality this is not unlike a croquette, so it can be used and served as such. However, I think this piece deserves a bit more "protocol": it could be presented already on a fork, for example.

Sauté the monkfish in a pan with a bit of oil.

Dip in the egg batter.

"Bread" with the dehydrated vegetables.

I am therefore in favor of discarding the term "miniature cuisine", because I do not like it and it seems inadequate. I would prefer to speak of cuisine adapted for "eating standing up" and keep traditional names without needing to rename the dishes.
I would rather that the preparations be part of the surprise of the party—that when a server offers a tray of *escudella i carn d'olla**, the guest accept the item with a smile and a look of satisfaction, appreciating not only the originality but also the effort and desire put into its preparation.
And of course, and this is perhaps most important, that after tasting it he or she identify without question the flavors of the original dish. That there not be deviations in taste. That is, that the guest will have the sensation and be convinced of eating *escudella i carn d'olla**.

"Escudella i carn d'olla" for cocktail parties

Ingredients (for 10 servings)

- 1/4 gal. *escudella*
- 10 *escudella i carn d'olla** brochettes

"Escudella i carn d´olla"

(yields approximately 1 gal.)

Ingredients

For the *escudella i carn d'olla*

17-1/2 oz. veal shank
1/2 hen
7 oz. pig's ears and snout
1 pig's foot
6 oz. salted fresh lard
1 piece blood pudding (approx. 11 oz.)
pork and beef bones
1 cabbage
2 medium carrots
1 turnip
2 large potatoes
1 large onion
9 oz. chickpeas, soaked overnight

For the meatball

5-1/2 oz. lard
5-1/2 oz. lean pork
1 egg
2 slices white bread
2 tsp. finely chopped garlic and parsley
2 tsp. pine nuts
2 tsp. flour
milk
salt
pepper

METHOD

1. *Clean and dress the pieces of meat (except for the blood pudding), washing them if necessary.*
2. *Place them in a 2-gallon pot, fill with 1-1/2 gallon of water and bring to a boil.*
3. *When it reaches a boil, add the chickpeas and simmer for 2 hours over low heat.*
4. *Meanwhile, prepare the meatballs in the following way:*
   a) Run the meat through a grinder.
   b) Add the bread soaked in milk and the rest of the ingredients.
   c) Make small meatballs.

   Note: In the traditional recipe, the meatballs would be bigger and they would be added at the same time as the vegetables.

   d) Roll in flour and refrigerate until use.
5. *Add the blood pudding and vegetables, chopped into medium-sized pieces.*
6. *When the vegetables begin to soften, add the meatballs and cook for 5 more minutes, then remove from heat.*
7. *Separate the bouillon (*escudella*) from the meat, vegetables and chickpeas (*carn d'olla*). Of the resulting bouillon, set aside 1/4 gallon for this recipe and keep the rest for other uses.*

"ESCUDELLA I CARN D´OLLA" BROCHETTE

INGREDIENTS

The meats, vegetables, legumes and meatballs from the escudella i carn d'olla *recipe.*

METHOD

1. *Cut small pieces, to taste, of all of the* carn d'olla *ingredients.*
2. *Use 5-in. bamboo skewers to prepare brochettes with the ingredients. Put on the meatball last.*

Note: all of the ingredients of the *carn d'olla* need not be on the brochette, but it should be a combination that evokes the dish. I recommend preparing it with one or two representative elements from each group; that is, one piece of meat, one vegetable, one legume and a meatball. Keep in mind that this skewer will be served in a small cup filled with the bouillon from the *escudella*.

ASSEMBLY

1. Place the skewers inside small cups at room temperature.
2. Cover with the boiling *escudella* and serve.

Note: servers should advise guests to first eat the brochette, then drink the broth.

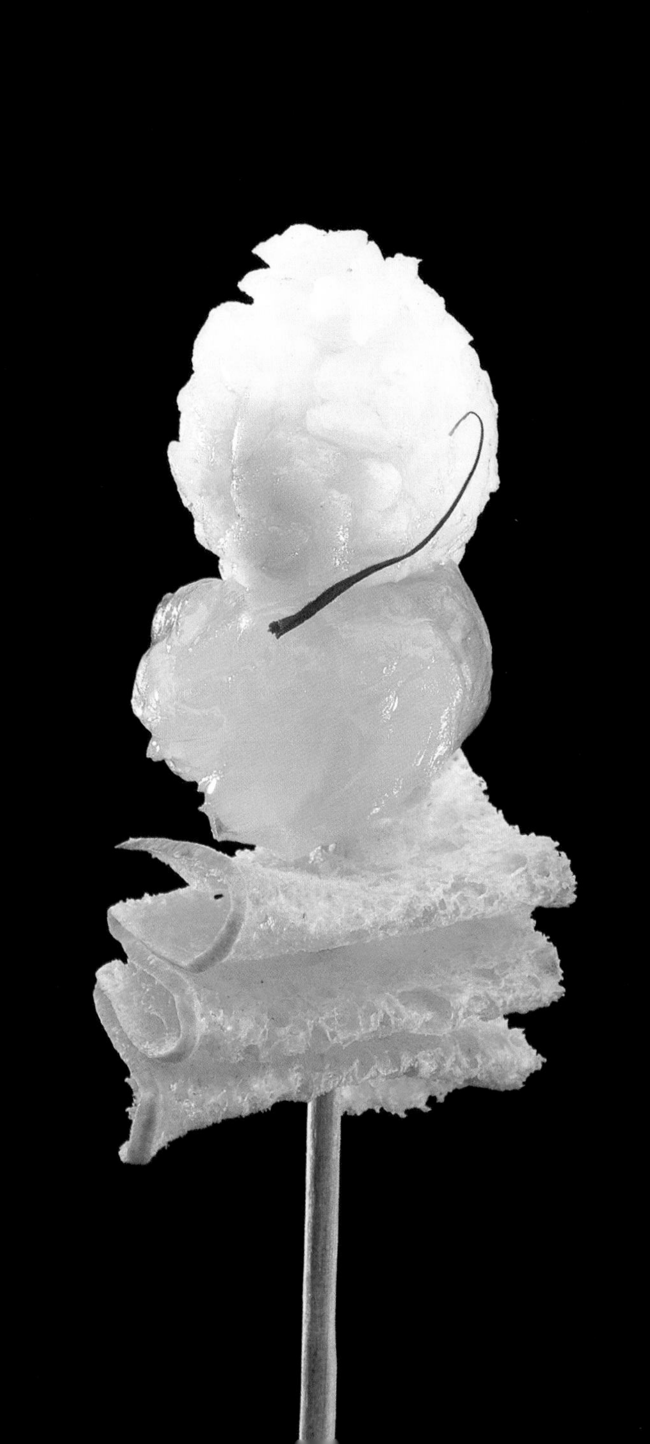

Spiny lobster "caldereta" for cocktail parties

Ingredients (for 10 servings)

- 1 qt. spiny lobster *caldereta** stock
- 10 spiny lobster, toast and rice brochettes

Spiny lobster "caldereta" stock

Ingredients

6-1/2 lbs. spiny lobster heads (separate the tails for the brochette portions)
1 pint olive oil
2-3/16 lbs. onion
2-3/16 lbs. grated fresh tomato (salted and sweetened with sugar)
1 large red pepper (or 2 small ones)
1 tbsp. garlic cloves (half of one for mixing with the parsley)
1 tbsp. dark chocolate, chopped with a knife
parsley
mineral water
salt

Method

1. *Cut the heads in half, saving the juice and small pieces of flesh that separate. If they have roe, set it aside.*
2. *Fry the heads, previously seasoned with the oil. Set aside.*
3. *Strain the oil and make a sauce base with the onion, pepper, tomato and garlic, all finely chopped or puréed.*
4. *Mix the sauce base with the heads and all of their juice. Set part of it aside.*
5. *Place in a clay pot over low heat and add water until it covers the ingredients.*
6. *While it simmers, blend the roe with the part of the juice previously set aside, the chocolate finely chopped with a knife, garlic and parsley. Add the mixture to the stock.*
7. *Allow to sit for 4 hours and strain through a conical strainer.*

Note: to prepare the stew as a dish rather than an appetizer, add the sliced tails in with the heads. 15 minutes before it is done cooking, add a cupful of rice. Serve with thin toast.

SPINY LOBSTER, TOAST AND RICE BROCHETTE

INGREDIENTS

Thin strips of par-baked bread (p. 52), about 4 in. long and 3/4 in. wide
Raw spiny lobster, cut into cubes 5/8 in. on a side.
(see ingredients for the Spiny lobster *caldereta* Stock, p. 121)
Makicanapés *rice (p. 151)*

METHOD

1. *Give the par-baked bread strip the shape of a small accordion, then skewer (leave enough room above it on the skewer for the lobster cube and a rice ball).*
2. *Toast in the oven at 320ºF (160ºC) on a silicone sheet until golden brown. Let cool at room temperature.*
3. *Skewer the lightly seasoned raw spiny lobster cube.*
4. *Shape the rice into a compact ball with your hands and skewer so that it is touching the lobster cube.*

Note: the spiny lobster cube will cook when the brochette is covered with the boiling stock.
The brochette must be put together so that the stock only covers the rice and the lobster. The toast must stay dry so that it does not soften.

ASSEMBLY

1. Heat the brochettes a bit in the oven before placing them inside the cups.
2. Pour the spiny lobster *caldereta* stock into a small pitcher and place it next to the cups on a tray.
3. Present the cup with the brochette inside and fill with stock just before serving. This assures that it keeps its characteristics.

Note: servers should advise guests to first eat the brochette, then drink the broth.

Fish "suquet" for cocktail parties

Ingredients (for 10 servings)

- 1 qt. *suquet** stock
- 10 *suquet** brochettes

"Suquet" stock

Ingredients

2-3/16 lbs. small coastal fish, sliced or cubed
4 large potatoes
1 onion
4 peeled seedless tomatoes
2 tsp. finely chopped garlic and parsley
1 slice of bread, fried
1 tsp. pine nuts, toasted
1 monkfish liver
1 qt. white wine
saffron, garlic, salt and olive oil

You will need fish stock, made by boiling the heads and other remaining parts of the small coastal fish after they are cut. I recommend adding crabs and clams.

METHOD

1. *Heat the oil in a clay pot.*
2. *Add the finely chopped garlic and parsley, the tomato crushed with your fingers and the finely chopped onion. Stir.*
3. *Add the potatoes, peeled and cut unevenly (broken apart) as for a stew.*
4. *Sauté the potatoes for a few minutes, cover them with the stock and cook at high heat for 10 minutes.*
5. *Then season the fish and add it to the pot, lower the heat and cook for 5 more minutes.*
6. *Just before turning off the heat, flavor with a mixture of a bit of garlic, the fried bread, saffron, monkfish liver (raw), oil and white wine, all well ground together with mortar and pestle.*
7. *After adding this mixture, take the pot by its handles and move it back and forth (do not stir with a spatula).*
8. *Drain the stock and separate the potatoes and fish.*

Note: if not using this recipe for an appetizer, omit this last step. The *suquet* should instead be allowed to rest for a few moments in the pot before serving.

"SUQUET" BROCHETTE

INGREDIENTS

The potatoes and fish from the suquet *(see above)*

METHOD

1. *Cut the potatoes and the fish into cubes 3/4 in. on a side.*
2. *Skewer the fish and potatoes, alternating until the skewer is full.*

Note: keep in mind that the brochette will be served in a small cup and should be covered by the *suquet* stock.

ASSEMBLY

1. Heat the brochettes a bit in the oven before placing them into cups.
2. Pour the *suquet* stock into a small pitcher and place it next to the cups on a tray.
3. Present the cup with the brochette inside and fill with stock just before serving. This assures that it keeps its characteristics.

Note: servers should advise guests to first eat the brochette, then drink the broth.

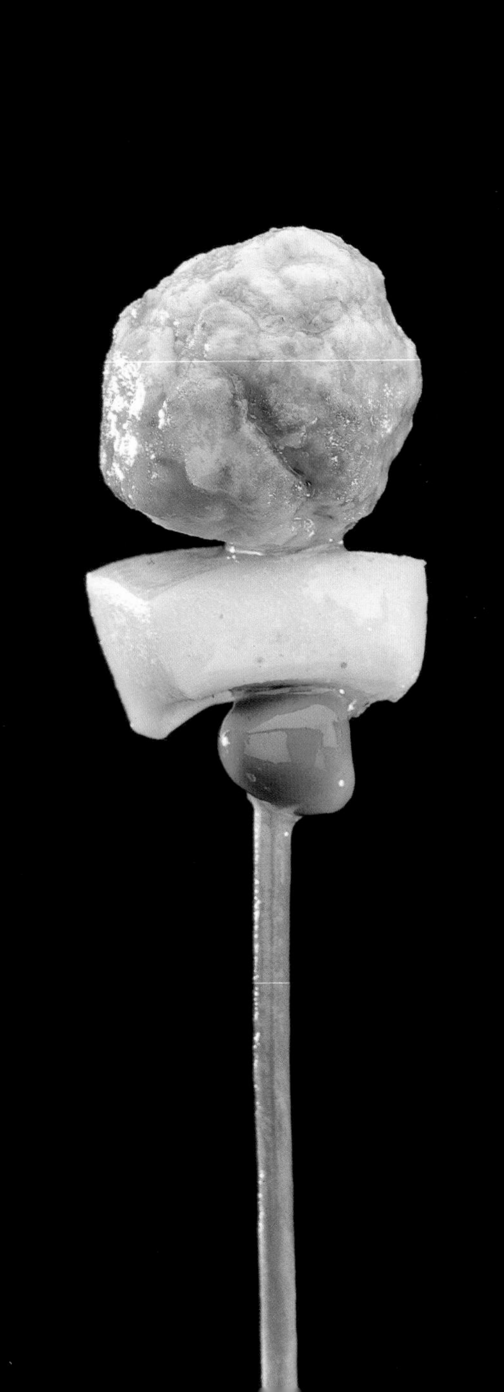

MEATBALLS WITH CUTTLEFISH FOR COCKTAIL PARTIES

INGREDIENTS (FOR 10 SERVINGS)

- 1 qt. meatball and cuttlefish stock
- 10 meatball and cuttlefish brochettes

MEATBALLS WITH CUTTLEFISH

INGREDIENTS

2-3/16 lbs. cleaned fresh cuttlefish
25 fried meatballs (approx. 3/4 in. in diameter)
10-1/2 oz. sauce base (finely chopped tomato and onion, sautéed in olive oil)
1 qt. seafood stock
3-1/2 fl oz. mellow wine
olive oil, salt

For the seasoning:

6 toasted almonds
1 garlic clove
parsley
1 tsp. dark chocolate
1 carquinyoli*

METHOD

1. *Cut the cuttlefish into cubes 3/4 in. on a side.*
2. *Brown it in a clay pot with oil.*
3. *Add the mellow wine, reduce heat for a few seconds.*
4. *Add the sauce base, stir and cover with the stock. Bring to a boil and reduce heat.*
5. *Salt to taste.*
6. *Fry the meatballs and add them to the stew.*
7. *Grind the seasoning mixture of almonds, garlic, parsley,* carquinyoli *and chocolate with a mortar and pestle.*
8. *Once the stew thickens, add the seasoning and continue cooking for a few minutes.*
9. *Strain the stock, separating the cuttlefish and meatballs.*

MEATBALL AND CUTTLEFISH BROCHETTE

INGREDIENTS

The meatballs, cuttlefish cubes and peas from the meatballs with cuttlefish recipe (p. 129)

METHOD

1. *Alternate skewering the meatballs, cuttlefish cubes and peas.*

Note: keep in mind that the brochette will be served in a small cup and should be covered by the stock.

ASSEMBLY

1. Place the brochettes into the cups at room temperature.
2. Fill with the boiling stock and serve.

Note: servers should advise guests to first eat the brochette, then drink the broth.

Spaghetti

I think pasta is one of the world's most ingenious foods. Its shapes, textures, versatility and taking on of whatever flavor it is given make this product something special.

Converting pasta into an hors d'oeuvre definitely had its glitches. As a rule, it is not something simple to eat: spaghetti should be served in a deep dish and eaten sitting down, with a certain level of dexterity with a fork so as to impart a proportional amount of sauce to each bite.

Preparing spaghetti to eat in one bite at a cocktail party required sacrificing some of its original characteristics. The main one is temperature: the pieces are served cold. Second is the nature of the sauce: despite offering the most traditional of flavors (four cheese, Bolognese, Napolitana, Carbonara and pesto), the base is always béchamel. This serves two essential purposes: on the one hand, it "supports" the pasta; and on the other, it tempers the flavor of the sauce. The texture of pesto, for example, does not allow us to shape individual pieces. If, however, it is prepared with butter instead of oil and then mixed with béchamel, it not only gains the necessary density to shape the piece but also imparts the flavor in a subtler way.

I experimented with a number of gelatins with varying results, and in the end arrived at the conclusion that béchamel was a good match as much for the pasta as for my goal.

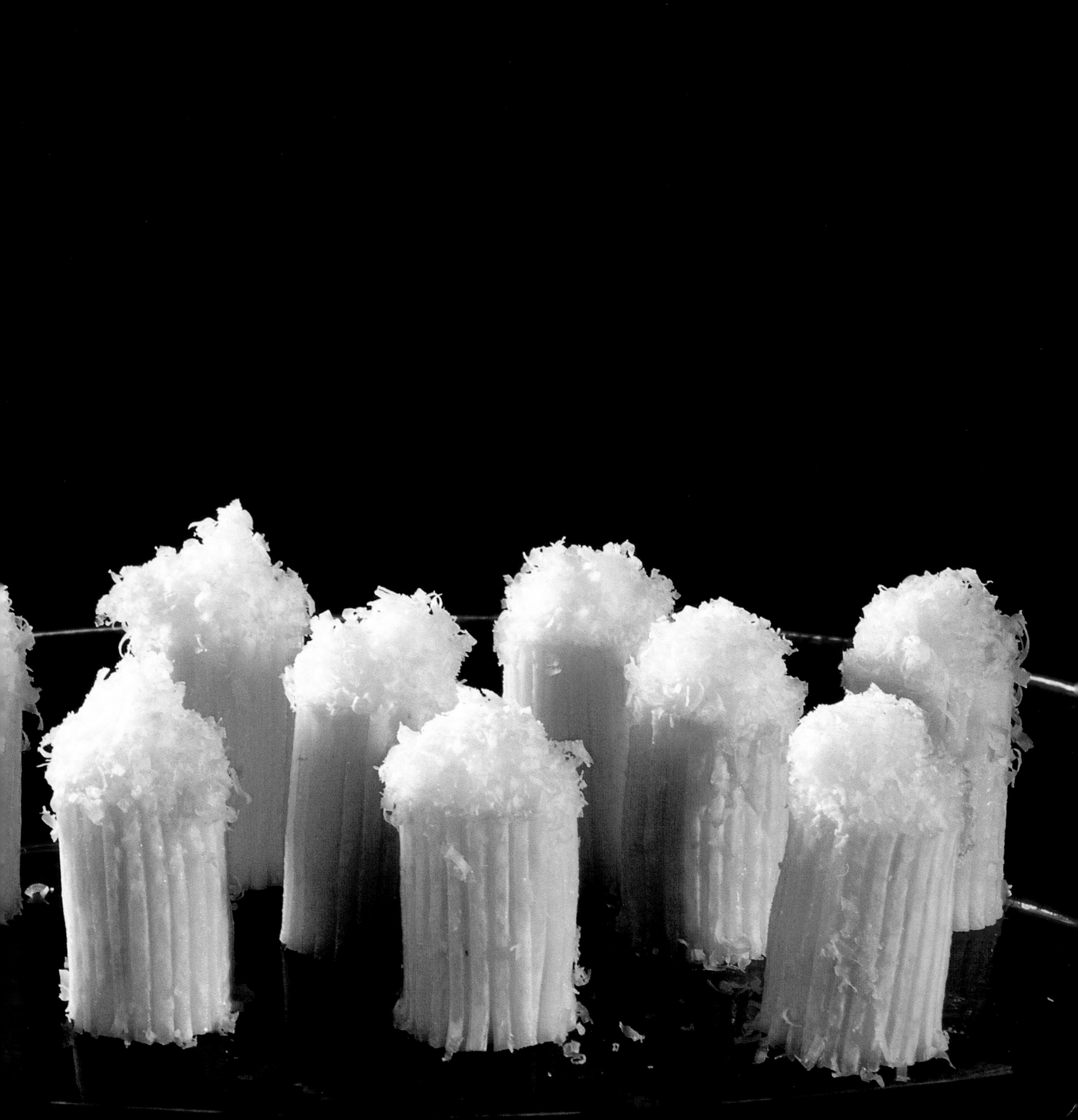

The technique

The technique for making these spaghetti "nuggets" is based on two main concepts: preparing a flavored béchamel and wrapping the sauce in pasta.

Flavored béchamel

The idea is simple: it consists of mixing the most traditional of pasta sauces with béchamel. This way, we end up with a shapeable and thick sauce that keeps all of its original flavor while tempering it at the same time. Be mindful never to blend these sauces in an electric blender because the béchamel will lose its consistency.

Béchamel Bolognese

Ingredients

24-1/2 oz. béchamel for croquettes (p. 198)
10-1/2 oz. Bolognese sauce

Method

1. *Drain as much of the oil as possible from the Bolognese sauce (I recommend doing this while hot).*
2. *Mix the two sauces while hot, then refrigerate.*

Béchamel Carbonara

Ingredients

24-1/2 oz. béchamel for croquettes (p. 198)
10-1/2 oz. Carbonara sauce

Method

1. *Mix the two sauces while hot, then refrigerate.*

Four Cheese Béchamel

Ingredients

24-1/2 oz. béchamel for croquettes (p. 198)
10-1/2 oz. thick four cheese sauce

Note: this is no more than a blend of your four cheeses of choice; one of which should always be a blue cheese, e.g. Cabrales, Gorgonzola, Roquefort, etc.

Method

1. *Mix the two sauces while hot, then refrigerate.*

Note: if the cheeses release fat in liquid form, stir when the sauce is almost cold to blend it in.

y out the spaghetti on a sheet of astic wrap and pipe the filling.

l up with the aid of the plastic wrap.

Finish shaping the cylinder.

Cut once frozen.

BÉCHAMEL NAPOLITANA

INGREDIENTS

24-1/2 oz. béchamel for croquettes (p. 198)
10-1/2 oz. tomato sauce
oregano

METHOD

1. *Drain as much of the oil as possible from the tomato sauce (I recommend doing this while hot).*
2. *Mix the two sauces while hot.*
3. *Add oregano to taste.*

PESTO BÉCHAMEL

INGREDIENTS

24-1/2 oz. béchamel for croquettes (p. 198)
10-1/2 oz. butter pesto (p. 195)

METHOD

1. *Mix the two sauces while hot.*

Wrapping sauce in pasta

Perhaps the easiest thing would have been to make cannelloni, fill them and cut them into cylinders. However, it was much more fun for me to imagine a cocktail party menu where one of the appetizers was spaghetti. So I decided to come up with a way to make that happen. Various attempts were made, and the one that worked the best was to lay out the already cooked spaghetti onto plastic wrap, pipe a cylinder of béchamel along the center with a pastry bag, roll it up and freeze it. It can also be done without freezing, but cutting it is more delicate. When it comes out of the freezer, it takes but a few minutes to make clean cuts without affecting the shape.

Spaghetti with Four Cheese Sauce

Ingredients (for 10 "nuggets")

- 25 spaghetti noodles, 10 in. in length
- 3 oz. four cheese béchamel (p. 134)
- Parmesan "snow"

Parmesan "snow"

Ingredients

3-1/2 oz. fresh Parmesan cheese

Method

1. *Grate the cheese with a very fine grater to make very finely shaved Parmesan. It is very important not to use cheese that is too dry.*

Note: avoid piling it up, compacting it, storing it under pressure, etc.

Method

1. On a flat surface, lay out the 25 spaghetti noodles in line and touching each other on a sheet of plastic wrap.
2. Using a pastry bag, pipe a cylinder of four cheese béchamel 3/8 in. in diameter the length of the spaghetti "mat".
3. Roll the plastic wrap to make a cylinder.
4. Freeze or refrigerate (I recommend freezing to make cutting easier).

Assembly

1. Cut the partly thawed cylinder into 1 in. long portions.
2. Serve vertically with a bit of Parmesan "snow" on top.

Note: to make spaghetti Bolognese, Napolitana, Carbonara and pesto, follow exactly the same steps using your béchamel of choice (pp. 134-145).

Spoonfuls

Once again, we find ourselves with an excellent means for serving various preparations at a cocktail party.

In this chapter, the container is almost more important than what it contains. I do not mean to say that the recipes I present are uninteresting, but I do want the idea of the utensil to take precedence over all else. My suggestions are merely examples of what these little spoons can hold; I hope they serve as inspiration and as a starting point for imagining an infinite number of preparations.

There is one detail that must be taken into account when working with these spoons: they are not adequate devices for serving hot foods. The main reason is that most spoons are made of china, porcelain or metal—all good heat conductors. If, to keep things hot, the spoons are heated in a plate warmer, oven or hot room just before being served, they will be too hot to the touch and may even burn the guest. If, on the other hand, the spoons are cold and filled just before serving, the food will cool very quickly, besides the inconvenience this creates. For these reasons, I recommend always using foods that are cold or at room temperature.

Spoonful of pumpkin, caviar and orange

Ingredients (for 10 spoonfuls)

- 3-1/2 oz. pumpkin purée
- 2 tbsp. caviar
- orange dust (p. 191)

Pumpkin purée

Ingredients

24-1/2 oz. pumpkin pulp
24-1/2 oz. butter
6-3/4 oz. cream
salt

Method

1. *Cook the pumpkin wrapped in aluminum foil or sous-vide in a steam oven.*
2. *Purée with the butter and cream.*
3. *Bring to a boil for a few minutes.*
4. *Refrigerate.*

Note: there is canned pumpkin purée available on the market (certain brands are of quite respectable quality) that can save time and work.

Assembly

1. Using a pastry bag with a tip cut into a point, pipe a small quenelle of pumpkin purée into the spoon.
2. Top with the caviar and sprinkle with a pinch of orange dust.
3. Serve very cold.

Shape a quenelle with a pastry bag.

Spoonful of Japanese Noodles and Salmon Roe

Ingredients (for 10 spoonfuls)

- 3-1/2 oz. Japanese *somen** noodles
- 2 tbsp. salmon roe
- sesame oil

* *Japanese wheat noodles. The most commonly used Japanese noodles are:* udon, soba, somen *and* chukamen. *In this recipe, I recommend using somen because they are the thinnest (see glossary).*

Method and Assembly

1. Boil the *somen* noodles for 1 minute; chill.
2. Place a "nest" of noodles in the spoon.
3. Top with the roe and drizzle with sesame oil.

Note: the somen *noodles can be kept in sesame oil once cooked.*

Spoonful of Green Tea with Asparagus

Ingredients (for 10 spoonfuls)

- 3-1/2 oz. green tea paste
- 1 oz. asparagus tips
- extra virgin olive oil

Green Tea Paste

Ingredients

1 tbsp. powdered green tea (ceremonial variety)
24-1/2 oz. cream
1-3/4 oz. sugar
2 gelatin sheets

Method

1. *Soak the gelatin in plenty of cold water.*
2. *Boil the cream with the powdered green tea and the sugar.*
3. *Drain the gelatin and heat in a saucepan.*
4. *Once melted, add part of the cream, green tea and sugar mixture. Stir well.*
5. *Mix in the rest of the mixture and refrigerate.*
6. *After a minimum of 4 hours, emulsify.*

Assembly

1. Using a pastry bag, pipe the green tea paste into the spoon.
2. Place the sautéed or blanched asparagus tips onto the paste.
3. Drizzle with extra virgin olive oil.

Note: this recipe is made for lovers of bitter flavors. Often, in a cocktail party or aperitif, it is difficult to discern the ingredients in certain items, and many times they remain unknown until tasted. For its peculiar flavor, this particular hors d'œuvre requires a bit of information before it is tasted.

Spoonful of miso with spring onion

Ingredients (for 10 spoonfuls)

- 3-1/2 oz. *miso** purée
- spring onion (to cut small rings)

Miso purée

Ingredients

14 oz. cream
4-1/2 oz. white miso *paste*
1 gelatin sheet

Method

1. *Soak the gelatin in plenty of water.*
2. *Drain and place in a saucepan over medium heat.*
3. *Add some of the cream and blend well.*
4. *Add the* miso *and the remaining cream. Stir until homogeneous.*
5. *Refrigerate for 12 hours. Emulsify.*

Assembly

1. Cut small spring onion rings and set aside in ice water.
2. Using a pastry bag with the tip cut to a point, pipe a small quenelle of *miso* purée into the spoon.
3. Top with a few spring onion rings.

MAKICANAPÉS

The Japanese word *maki* refers to a cylinder of rice wrapped in *nori** seaweed and filled with raw fish, meat or other ingredients in addition to the requisite *wasabi**. It is prepared by laying the seaweed onto a *makisu**, a sushi mat made of small bamboo sticks tied together with string. On top of the seaweed is placed the specially prepared rice (see p. 151), followed by strips of raw fish (one of the most common ingredients) laid in line and lightly brushed with *wasabi*. They roll it with the aid of the *makisu* and then cut it with a sharp knife, moistened with water or rice vinegar. Thus is made one of the most characteristic pieces in Japanese cuisine.

One of the most important elements for the success of these pieces is the technique for cooking the rice. From the just right washing of the grains to its cooling and airing in an untreated wood bowl so that it absorbs the moisture, followed by seasoning with sake, sugar, rice vinegar and *konbu** seaweed. The mastery of this technique yields rice with ideal characteristics for manipulating and eating cold.

According to Paco Guzmán, in my humble opinion a great expert in Asian cooking, preparing this type of rice must be done as with bread: the best way is for the same person to make it in the same place, with the same tools and, if possible, at the same time of day. The goal is for the designated person to master the intricacies of the process so that, with time, the rice comes out the way it should almost without thought.

Drawing inspiration from *maki* and canapés, I created the *makicanapé*, a simple and easy piece that combines the appearance of a canapé with the taste of *maki*. Here once again my obsession for not using bread as a base comes out, and I substitute it with what I've always considered to be East Asia's version of bread: rice.

The technique

I stress that the most important technique is preparing the rice; if unfamiliar with it at first, I recommend following the method described in these pages to the letter.

In the step-by-step photos for the recipes, note that to prepare the seaweed and rice base for the *makicanapés*, the original Japanese tools (*oshizushi**) are used along with the ancient technique, beautiful for its simplicity.

I also treat the soy sauce (p. 153) to give the piece shine and flavor. Without this final touch of soy sauce, the *makicanapé* ends up being "decaffeinated", or dull.

Preparing the *makicanapés* requires the use of many ingredients and utensils found in Japanese cooking. When in doubt, you may consult the glossary included at the end of this book.

Below you will find, in addition to the *makicanapé* rice, other necessary procedures and methods for following the recipes in this chapter.

Rice for makicanapés

Ingredients

3-1/2 oz. Japanese rice
1 piece konbu* *seaweed*
2 tbsp. mirin*
2 tbsp. rice vinegar
water (twice the volume of the rice)

Method

1. *Place the rice in a chinois and rinse with cold water under the tap at high pressure until the water filtered by the rice is completely clear.*
2. *Put the rice in a pot, cover with the water. Then add the* konbu, *previously washed with a moist towel, cover and let sit for at least 1/2 hour.*
3. *After this time, add the* mirin *and place over high heat.*
4. *Once boiling, remove the seaweed and cook in the oven at 320ºF (160ºC) for 20 minutes.*
5. *Spread out the rice over an untreated wood surface large enough to stir the rice while you add the vinegar. Fan the rice so that it cools faster.*
6. *Store in a container.*

MAKICANAPÉS

INGREDIENTS

Rice for makicanapés
Nori* *seaweed*

METHOD

1. *Cut the* nori *to the size of the* oshizushi.
2. *Moisten the* oshizushi *with cold water and put the pieces together.*
3. *Line the bottom with a* nori *strip.*
4. *Spoon in a 3/8 in. thick layer of rice.*
5. *Place another seaweed strip on top and press down with the moistened cover.*
6. *Remove the cover and cut into pieces with a very sharp, moistened knife through the slits in the* oshizushi.
7. *Remove the* oshizushi.

Utensils and ingredients.

Moisten the oshizushi *and put it together. Line the base with the cut seaweed and fill with rice.*

Cover with another nori *strip.*

Press down with the oshizushi *cover.*

Remove the cover and slice with a moistened knife along the slits in the oshizushi.

Remove the oshizushi.

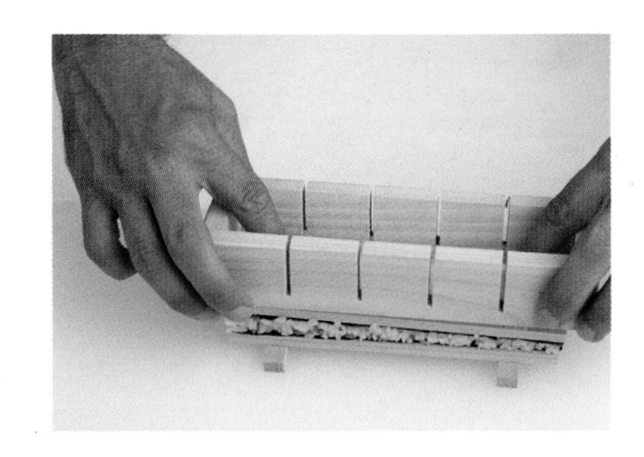

HERRING FOR MAKICANAPÉS

INGREDIENTS

Very fresh herrings
Salt
Rice vinegar

METHOD

1. *Separate the two filets and remove all of the bones from the herrings.*
2. *Wash and dry.*
3. *Line the base of a container with salt, lay the filets on top and cover with salt. Allow to sit for 1 hour. This process makes the thin transparent film that covers the herring skin easy to remove and makes the skin edible and pleasant.*
4. *Marinate for 20 minutes in the rice vinegar.*

WASABI GELATIN

INGREDIENTS

4 tsp. wasabi
7 oz. mineral water
1 gelatin sheet

METHOD

1. *Pour the cold water into a saucepan and add the* wasabi.
2. *Place over low heat and stir.*
3. *When it starts to boil, skim the foam from the top, then strain.*
4. *Add the gelatin sheet, previously soaked in plenty of cold water, and dissolve completely.*
5. *Pour the mixture into a container and allow to gel in the refrigerator.*

SOY GLAZE

INGREDIENTS

7 oz. soy sauce
2 tbsp. neutral pastry glaze

METHOD

1. *Blend the soy sauce with the neutral glaze and refrigerate until use.*

Note: pastry glazes are gelatins of a creamy texture used to coat cakes so as to make them shiny and vibrant. There are neutral and flavored glazes. The flavored ones are rather sweet and, mixed with soy sauce (salty), are also good for items like the *makicanapés* I present in the following pages. A flavored glaze can therefore be used in the absence of a neutral one.

SHRIMP MAKICANAPÉ

INGREDIENTS (FOR 12 PIECES)

- 12 *makicanapé* pieces (p. 152)
- 4 very fresh large red shrimp
- 12 drops *wasabi* gelatin (p. 153)
- 1/2 tsp. pickled ginger
- 1-1/2 tbsp. soy glaze (p. 153)

ASSEMBLY

1. Peal the shrimp and cut them into three about equal pieces.
2. Place the *makicanapés* on a metal cake grid with a tray underneath.
3. Arrange a piece of shrimp in the center of each *makicanapé*.
4. Top with the *wasabi* gelatin and a small slice of ginger.
5. Coat with the soy glaze.

Note: to make the tuna, salmon and salmon roe makicanapés, *follow the same procedure; but for the herring* makicanapé, *the fish must be prepared beforehand (see the recipe for "herring for* makicanapé", *p. 153).*
The photos on pp. 148 and 149 show an assortment of makicanapés, *in which various cuts and products have been combined to taste.*

Ribs

With a little ingenuity, ribs can be made into remarkable pieces that are perfect for serving at a cocktail party. It simply requires taking advantage of the bone, whether in meat or fish, and using it as a skewer. Once clean, a little imagination here can go a long way.

Picture, for example, a kid rib—the well-polished bone can serve as a handle. The same bone can also make for more complex presentations if used as a skewer for inserting other ingredients to accompany the meat.

Less common are fish ribs. Opening up a sea bass to cut individual pieces and serve them on trays like ribs: this peculiar way to serve fish at a cocktail party is sure to surprise more than one guest. Though the process might seem complicated, and is to a certain extent, the results are phenomenal.

In this chapter I present a series of preparations that illustrate the possibilities for ribs as hors d'œuvres.

The technique

The three techniques applied in this chapter are separating the ribs of a sea bass, those of a turkey carcass, and using the bone from a rabbit rib to skewer ingredients.
I would not like to confuse idea with technique, as gastronomically close as they might be to one another. I see separating the ribs from a sea bass as more of a technique than an idea, or at most the sum of the two. Using a rabbit rib bone as a skewer for other ingredients, however, is more of an idea than a technique.
When I decided on trying fish ribs, the first type that came to mind was salmon. Though it is quite common, it offered many possibilities because it can be served hot or cold: from raw ribs served as sushi or marinated, to fried or grilled ribs. However, I found myself with a bone that was too soft and too thin and did not adequately serve the function I was looking for, which in this case was to support the meat.
So I had to choose a fish with optimal natural characteristics for making ribs. They also had to be sufficiently dense and rigid, and had to really look like ribs. The best option I came across was a large sea bass. Thanks to its hard, long, defined and visible bones I was able to achieve my goal; not only did they look like ribs, but they served their function perfectly. What stands out among the virtues of this piece is its integrity, gastronomically speaking, in that it does not lose the gelatin from the bones. Also notable is the fact that it allows for fun presentations, with or without building, and it is easy to eat, as much with utensils as with one's hands.
Indeed, these ribs could go from being an hors d'œuvre to being a dish on a restaurant menu if served on a plate. We should note that many of the recipes presented in this book as hors d'œuvres can easily be extrapolated to be served as dishes with the proper adaptation.

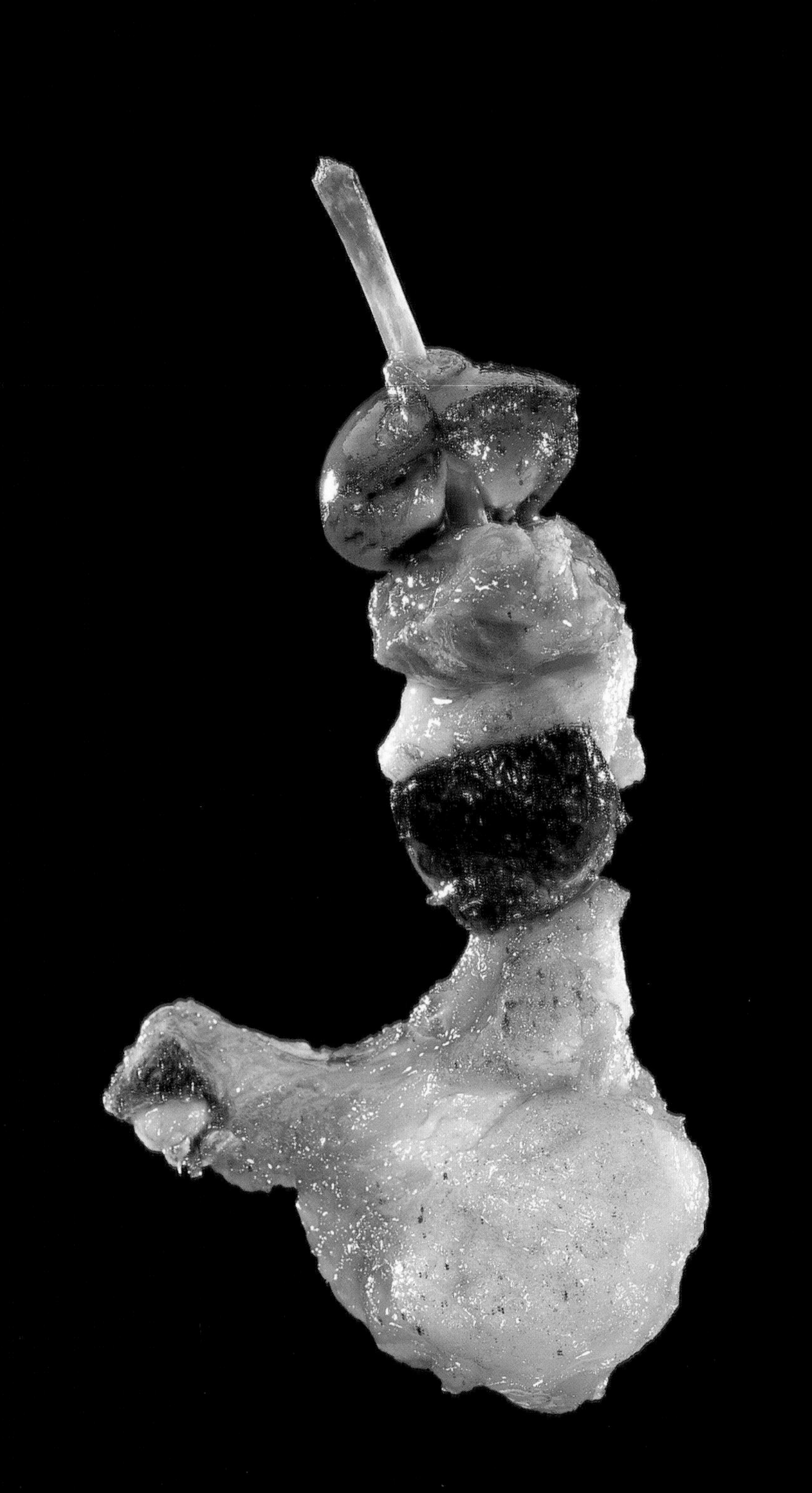

Rabbit ribs with salmorejo

Ingredients (for 8 pieces)

- 1 large rabbit's rack, with its head
- *salmorejo** sauce
- salt

Salmorejo sauce
(without marinating the rabbit meat)

Ingredients

3/4 qt. white wine
1/4 qt. red wine vinegar
1/4 qt. olive oil
15 garlic cloves
1/2 tsp. freshly ground black pepper
1/2 tsp. ground chili pepper
1/2 tsp. paprika
1 pinch thyme leaves
1 pinch oregano leaves
coarse grain salt
bones and trimmings (obtained from de-boning two rabbits)
beef stock

Method

1. *Mash the garlic with the salt and pepper to make a paste. Add the chili pepper and paprika.*
2. *Add the wine and vinegar. Gradually pour in the oil while stirring to emulsify and make a smooth sauce.*
3. *Move the mixture to a pot and add the thyme and oregano. Mix in the rabbit bones and trimmings and allow to marinate.*
4. *Lightly brown the marinated bones and trimmings.*
5. *Roast them in the oven. Once removed and while still very hot, stir the rabbit bones and trimmings once again into the pot with the marinade.*
6. *Cover with beef stock and simmer over low heat for 2 hours.*
7. *Very finely strain.*

METHOD

1. Separate the tenderloin, the kidneys, liver and the cheek from the rabbit.
2. Cut each rib and clean the bone, leaving it well polished (a rabbit's rack yields 8 ribs for this use).
3. Cut the tenderloin, kidneys, liver and cheek into small pieces.
4. Make a brochette with these pieces or skewer them on the rib bones.
5. Grill or fry in a pan with a bit of oil.
6. Coat with the salmorejo sauce or serve it on the side.

Note: for this piece the recipe for rabbit with Salmorejo *has been adapted—the original recipe calls for marinating the rabbit meat in the sauce before stewing.*

Rack and clean pieces.

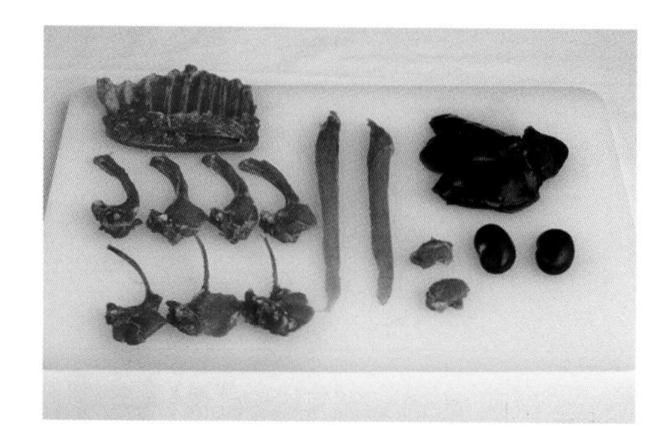

Cuts and preparation.

Turkey ribs with soy caramel sauce

Ingredients (for 12 pieces)

- 1 large turkey carcass
- 3-1/2 tbsp. burnt sugar
- 3-1/2 tbsp. soy sauce
- 1 pint white brine
- salt

White brine

Ingredients

28 oz. olive oil
7 oz. white vinegar
1/2 garlic head
2 bay leaves
1 twig fresh thyme
4 black peppercorns
1 onion, julienned
14 oz. bouillon

Method

1. *Stew all of the ingredients except the vinegar and bouillon over low heat.*
2. *Add the bouillon and half of the vinegar and raise the heat for a few minutes.*
3. *Remove from heat and slowly add the rest of the vinegar until you obtain the desired flavor.*

Note: this brine must be stirred before use because the vinegar sinks to the bottom.

METHOD

1. Remove the ribcage and cut out the ribs (each turkey carcass yields 12 ribs for this use).
2. Salt the ribs, place in a container and cover in the boiling brine. Allow to cool, then drain.
3. Reduce the sugar with the soy sauce and, once thickened, add the ribs and coat well.
4. For serving, arrange the ribs into a small pile and top with the remaining sauce.

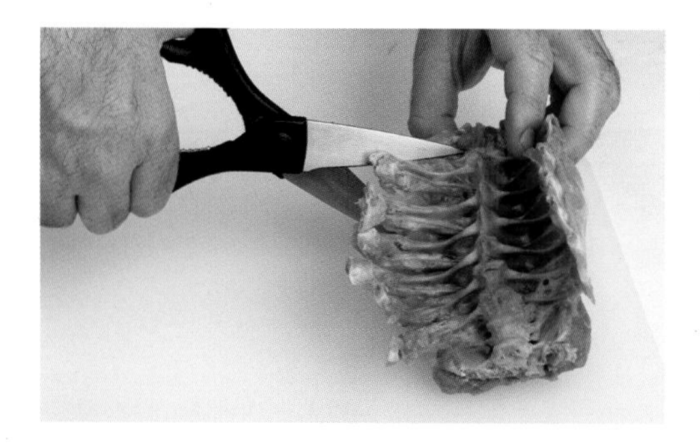

Start cutting out the ribs with scissors.

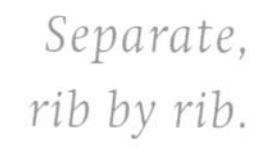

Separate, rib by rib.

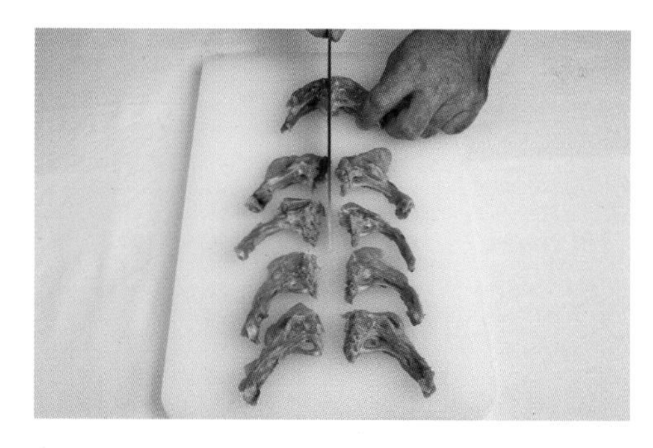

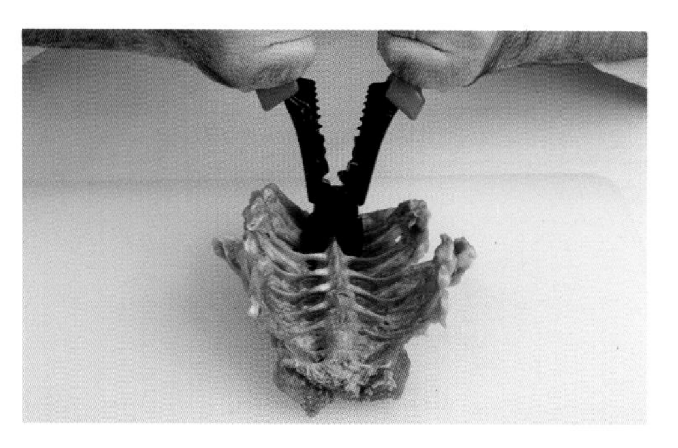

Cut the spine with pincers.

Marinate the ribs in the brine.

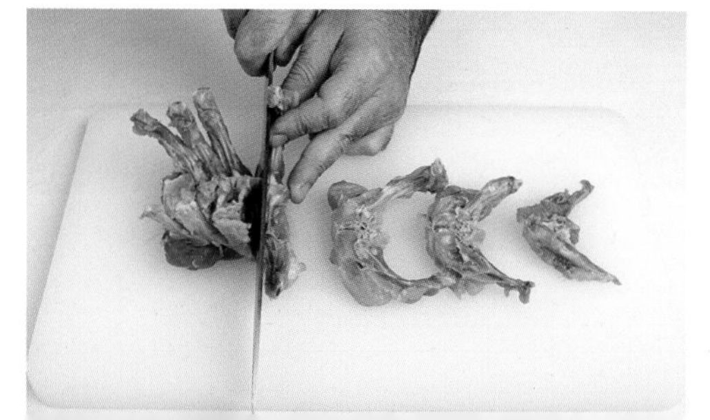

Finish cutting with a knife.

Cook with the soy caramel sauce.

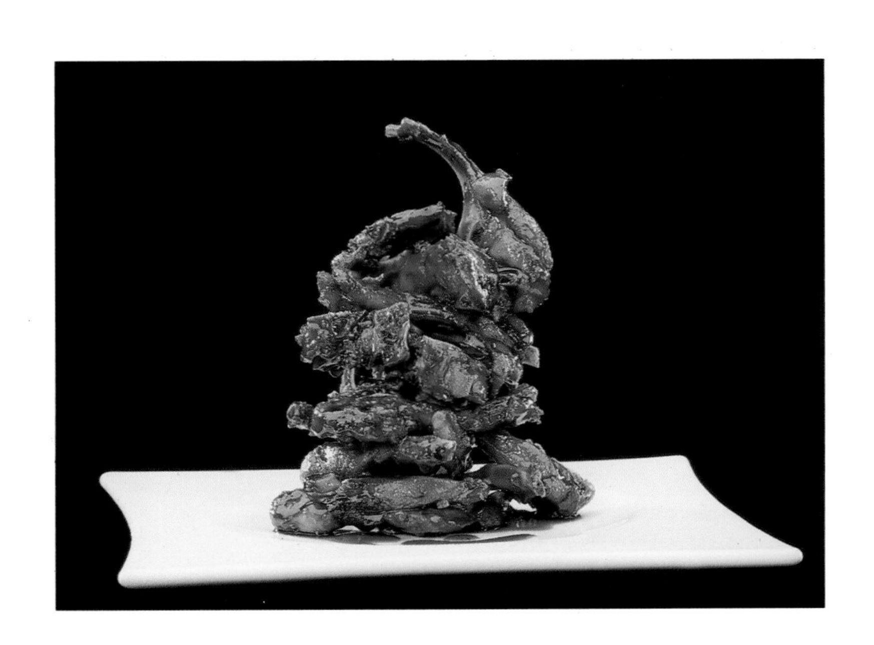

Santurce-style sea bass ribs

Ingredients (for 10 pieces)

- 1 large sea bass (minimum 4 lbs.)
- *Santurce* sauce
- olive oil
- salt

Santurce sauce

Ingredients

4 tbsp. olive oil
4 tbsp. butter
4 garlic cloves
1 cayenne pepper
2 tsp. sherry vinegar
4 tbsp. beef stock

Method

1. *Slice the peeled garlic cloves.*
2. *Sauté with the cayenne pepper in the oil until lightly brown.*
3. *Add the vinegar and allow to cool.*
4. *Strain through a chinois, pressing the garlic slices. Emulsify the sauce with the butter and beef stock.*

Note: if you do not need to use this sauce right away, I recommend thickening it with a bit of starch.

METHOD

1. Cut the sea bass into three pieces: the head, the section with the stomach cavity, and the rest with the tail.

Note: for this recipe use only the ventrêche *(belly) rather than the whole fish. Taking into account the price of this fish, the rest should be used; otherwise, the price of each rib is astronomical.*

2. Cut out the ribs following the steps described in the photo sequence.
3. Clean the resulting pieces, removing the excess meat from the upper part of the bone to give them the shape of a rib and leave them clean enough to pick up with one's fingers.
4. Drizzle with oil, salt and lightly grill.
5. Serve as is or with the *Santurce* sauce on top or on the side.

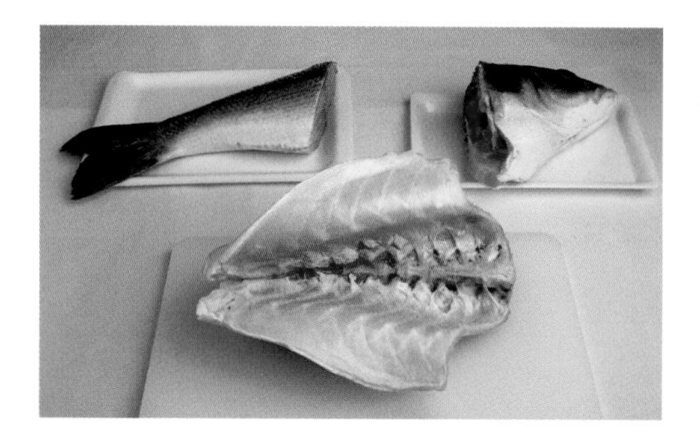

Sea bass in three sections.

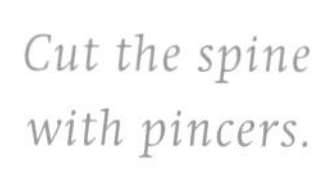

Cut the spine with pincers.

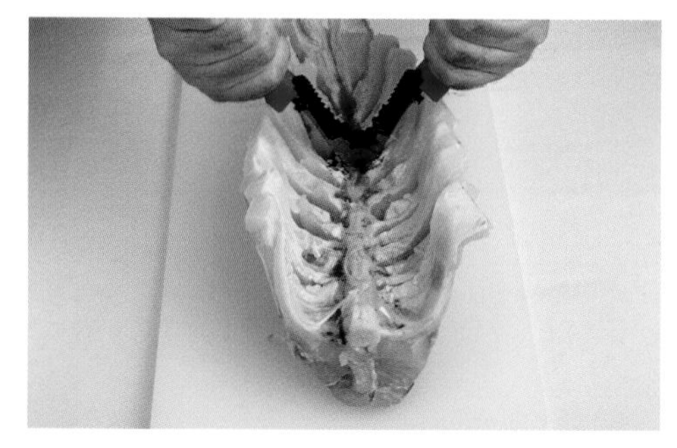

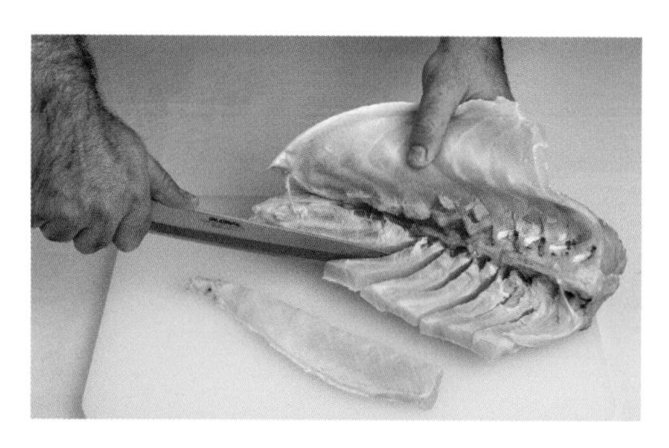

Cut with a knife from the inside.

Finish cutting with a knife.

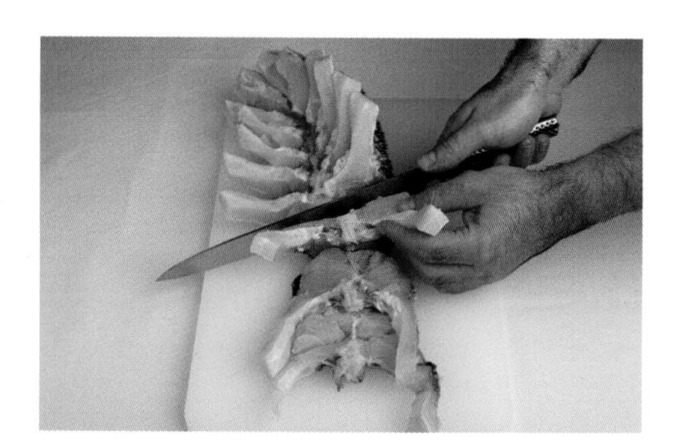

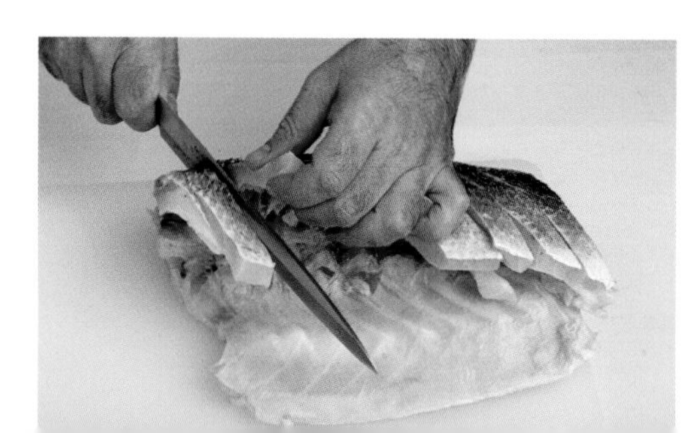

Continue from the outside.

Separate, rib by rib.

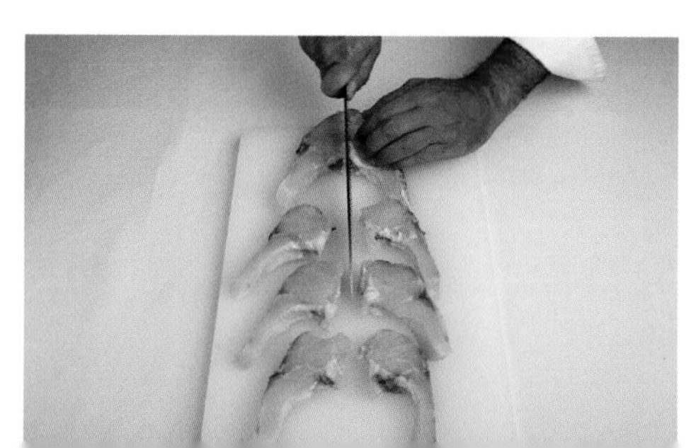

BREADED KID

INGREDIENTS (FOR 12 PIECES)

- 1 rack of kid
- 2 oz. cheese and mint filling
- 3-1/2 oz. whole eggs, beaten
- breadcrumbs
- flour
- salt

CHEESE AND MINT FILLING

INGREDIENTS

14 oz. solid fresh cheese, drained
3-1/2 oz. butter
2 garlic cloves, finely chopped (about 1-1/2 tsp.)
1 bunch fresh mint, finely chopped

METHOD

1. *Purée all of the ingredients to make a smooth, homogenous mixture.*
2. *Refrigerate.*

METHOD

1. Cut each rib and clean the bone, leaving it well polished.
2. With a meat flattener, carefully flatten the meat to make it thinner.
3. Place a ball of mint and cheese filling in the center of the meat. Wrap the filling in the meat and use the bone to keep it in place.
4. Season.
5. Coat each one in flour, egg and breadcrumbs.
6. Freeze or refrigerate for a few hours before frying.

Sequence of steps.

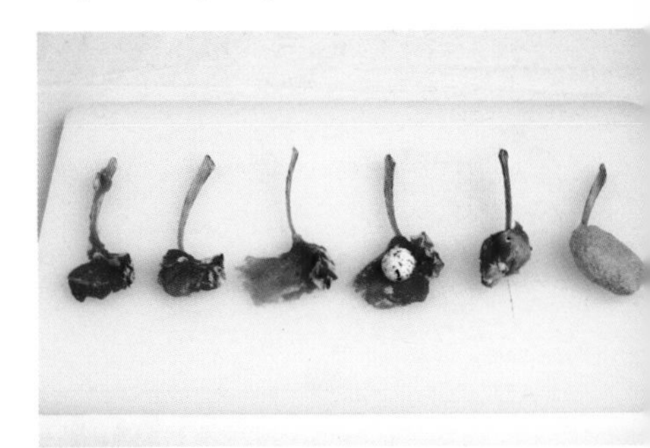

Additional Hors D'œuvres

This chapter contains four pieces that do not fit the criteria established for grouping the rest of the recipes. I thought it worthwhile to include them in a collection of this type and decided to classify them under the title "Additional Hors D'œuvres".

The crispy raw shrimp is one of the items of which I am most proud. The reason is that, apart from having an unconditional love for the Catalan coastal red shrimp, until now I only knew one way to prepare them without damaging the ingredient: in the pan (and I clearly still find it to be the best way). However, raw shrimp is delicious, and through the technique I outline here, the whole shrimp is eaten without damaging it. And when I say whole, I mean whole: head, tail and shell.

The other three pieces are easier to prepare, but they have certain qualities that make them especially attractive: one for its presentation, another for suggesting a new way to prepare every-day ingredients, and the last one for its application of the *sous-vide* technique.

With the murex, all I did was to slowly boil it in oil instead of water. Actually, it was stewed in oil and the shell was used as a base.

The crispy vegetable dumpling could perhaps have been included in the Fried Morsels chapter, but the special procedure it requires made it seem more fitting here. The preparation involves finely chopping grilled vegetables with blood sausage and mushrooms, then wrapping the mixture in a slice of par-baked bread to give it the shape of a small sausage. It is then fried and served with a mild *romesco** sauce.

The uniqueness of the rice chips comes in the use of the *sous-vide* technique. And though the preparation is relatively easy, it cannot be done as I explain here without using a vacuum sealer. The rest of the process does not present any complications as long as the quantities, times and temperatures are respected.

Crispy grilled vegetable dumplings

Ingredients (for 10 pieces)

- 10 thin slices of par-baked baguette
- 3-1/2 oz. finely chopped grilled vegetables and blood sausage
- 3-1/2 tbsp. *romesco** sauce (p. 196)
- olive oil for frying

Finely chopped grilled vegetables and blood sausage

Ingredients

10-1/2 oz. grilled vegetables
2 oz. Porcini mushrooms
(Boletus edulis)
3 oz. blood sausage
oil
salt

Method

1. *Using a knife, very finely chop the vegetables (previously fire-grilled).*
2. *Sauté the mushrooms, cut into large dice, in a non-stick pan with oil until golden brown. Chop them as with the vegetables.*
3. *Crumble the blood sausage.*
4. *Sauté the vegetables, mushrooms and blood sausage together with a bit of oil, stirring occasionally.*
5. *Refrigerate until use.*

Method

1. Place a spoonful of the chopped mixture onto the bread slice.
2. Wrap to give the shape of a small sausage.
3. Fry in hot oil until the bread is golden brown. Drain on absorbent paper for a few minutes.
4. Serve with *romesco* sauce.

Murexes with romesco

Ingredients (for 25 pieces)

- 25 large murexes
- 1/4 qt. stewing oil (p. 204)
- 3-1/2 oz. *romesco** sauce (p. 196)

Method

1. Place the murexes, previously washed in plenty of cold water, in a saucepan over very low heat and cover with the stewing oil.
2. Simmer for 45 minutes and let cool while still in the oil.
3. Remove the murexes from their shells and discard the undesired parts.

Assembly

1. Insert the clean murex into the point of its shell.
2. Brush with *romesco* sauce before serving.

Rice chips

Ingredients

- 7 oz. Japanese sushi rice
- 2 oz. *mirin**
- 1 oz. soy sauce
- 4-1/2 oz. mineral water

Method

1. Wash the rice by putting it in a fine-mesh sieve and running high-pressure cold water over it until the water passing through the rice is completely clear (at first it is cloudy). Drain.
2. Spoon into a *sous-vide* pouch together with the rest of the ingredients.
3. Vacuum seal.
4. Cook in a steam oven at 212ºF (100ºC) or in boiling water for 25 minutes. Let cool.
5. Once cold, open the bag and thinly slice.

Note: slice with a slicer or knife.
After making some slices, rinse the blade with cold water to remove the starch left by the rice.

6. Fry in oil at 284ºF (140ºC) until golden. Drain excess oil from the chips.

Note: before serving, lightly drizzle the chips with soy sauce. They are delicious!

CRISPY RAW SHRIMP

INGREDIENTS (FOR 10 PIECES)

- 10 medium red shrimp (Palamós variety)
- 3-1/2 oz. simple syrup (p. 204)
- sesame oil
- Maldon sea salt

METHOD

1. Separate the heads from the shrimp tails.
2. Run the heads through the blender and refrigerate the resulting juice at 37ºF (3ºC).
3. Using a pair of small curved cosmetic scissors, cut the shell between the legs so that the tail can be removed whole without damaging the shell.
4. De-vein the shrimp.
5. Dry the shrimp with a dry cloth.
6. Marinate the tails in sesame oil with Maldon sea salt in a covered container for a minimum of 2 hours.
7. Dip the whole shells in the syrup and caramelize in the oven on a silicone sheet at 356ºF (180ºC) for about 30 minutes.
8. Once the shells are cold and crispy, re-insert the shrimp into their shells and use the juice from the heads as a sauce.

Note: surprisingly, the whole shrimp is edible. The very crispy texture on the outside together with the indescribable inside are complemented perfectly by the flavor of the juice from the head. This technique and presentation offer a new way to eat shrimp, with the greatest respect for the ingredient.

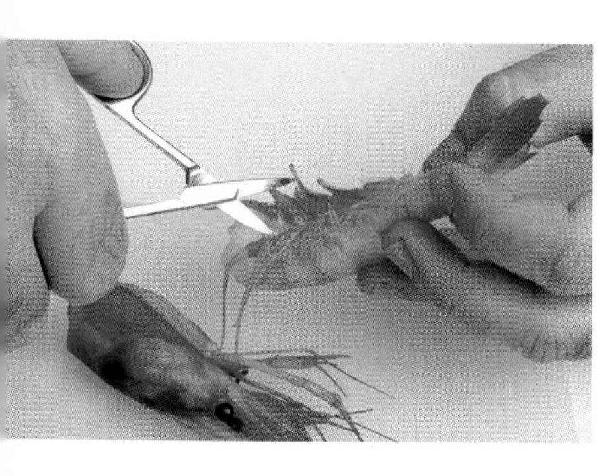

Cut with scissors.

Head, tail and shell.

Marinate the tails.

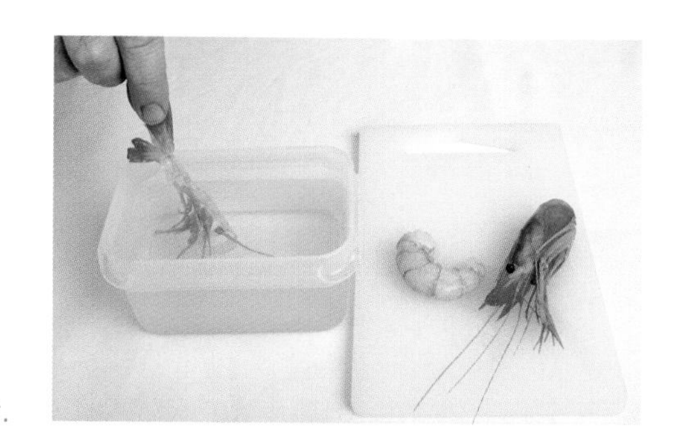

Dip the shells.

Place on a silicone sheet and into the oven.

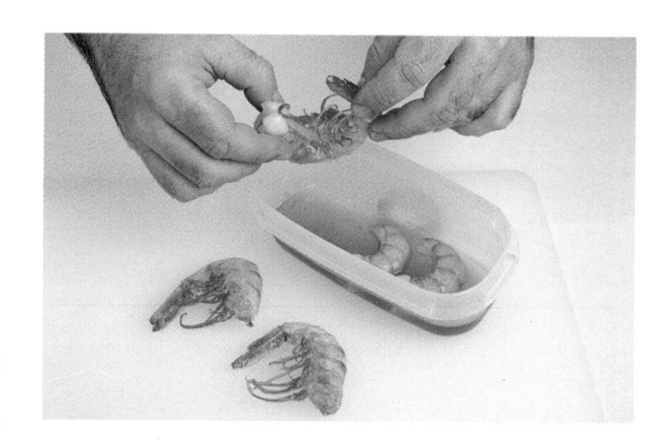

Re-insert the tails into the shells.

Basic recipes

Gelatins

Soy glaze

Ingredients

- 1/2 pint soy sauce
- 1 oz. neutral pastry glaze

Method

1. Blend the soy sauce with the neutral glaze and refrigerate until use.

Note: pastry glazes are gelatins of a creamy texture used to coat cakes so as to make them shiny and vibrant. There are neutral and flavored glazes. The flavored ones are rather sweet and, mixed with soy sauce (salty), are also good for items like the makicanapés. *A flavored glaze can therefore be used in the absence of a neutral one.*

Truffle gelatin

Ingredients

- 1/2 pint truffle juice
- 1 gelatin sheet

Method

1. Strain the truffle juice.
2. Soak the gelatin sheet in plenty of cold water.
3. Once hydrated, drain and place in a saucepan over low heat with two spoonfuls of truffle juice.
4. When the gelatin has melted completely, stir in the rest of the truffle juice.
5. Pour into a flat-bottom metal container to a maximum thickness of 1/4 in.
6. Allow to gel in the refrigerator.
7. Once gelled, cut into 1/4 in. strips and square them off to make cubes 1/4 in. on the one side.

Wasabi Gelatin

Ingredients

- 1 tsp. *wasabi**
- 1/2 pint mineral water
- 1 gelatin sheet

Method

1. Pour the cold water into a saucepan and add the *wasabi*.
2. Place over low heat and stir.
3. When it starts to boil, skim the foam from the surface, then strain.
4. Add the gelatin sheet, previously soaked in plenty of cold water, and melt completely.
5. Pour the mixture into a container and allow to gel in the refrigerator.

Dusts, powders, crocantis

Chicken skin crocanti

Ingredients

- One rotisserie chicken's skin

Method

1. Lay out the skin onto a silicone sheet.
2. Dry with a crumpled paper towel, pressing it onto the skin.
3. Top with another silicone sheet and toast in the oven at 320ºF (160ºC) for about 30 minutes until golden brown.
4. Remove from the oven and allow the skin to cool on a non-stick sheet.
5. Once cool and crispy, chop finely with a knife.

Note: if when cool it is not crispy, place again in the oven. Some parts of the skin may still not be crispy; in this case, discard them and use only the crispy pieces.

6. Store in an airtight container with a moisture absorber.

Powdered licorice

Ingredients

- 10-1/2 oz. licorice rocks
  (these rocks are usually sold by weight and shouldn't be confused with small black bars sold in candy stores, made with licorice but from which you cannot make powder).

Method

1. Place the rocks in the Thermomix container and grind at power level 12.
2. Sift through a fine-mesh sieve.
3. Store the powder in an airtight container protected from moisture.

Note: because they are very hard, never use a blender to grind the licorice rocks.

Orange dust

Ingredients

- 1 whole orange
- 1 pint mineral water
- 5-1/2 oz. sugar
- 3-1/2 oz. glucose

Method

1. Puncture the orange and place it in a saucepan, then cover with cold water.
2. Place over low heat. When it begins to boil, remove the orange and chill in the refrigerator.

Note: this process takes out some of the bitterness of the orange. It is actually an infusion, though in this case the said infusion is discarded for its bitterness, and the ingredient (the orange) is used devoid of one of its characteristics (the bitterness of the peel).

3. Boil the water with the sugar and glucose. Once they have dissolved, add the orange and reduce heat. Simmer for 2-1/2 hours, drain and cool.
4. Wrap in plastic and freeze.
5. Once completely frozen, remove the plastic wrap and grate very finely over wax paper, making sure to spread out the resulting powder as much as possible without piling it.
6. Allow to dry for a few hours in a warm place.
7. Store in a covered container and protect from moisture.

Note: this is a good technique for candying oranges, although using this recipe for eating the candied orange requires raising the sugar quantity by 2 oz. and storing it cold in its cooking syrup until serving.

Truffle dust

Ingredients

- Fresh truffles (*Tuber melanosporum*), or, if unavailable, canned ones

Method

1. Very finely grate over paper.
2. Allow to dry.
3. Store in an airtight container protected from moisture until use.

Reductions

The density of vinegar and liqueur reductions depends mainly on the type and quantity of the product, as well as the time it is boiled.
The following recipes give approximations so as to yield certain densities at room temperature that make these reductions neither too thin nor too thick. However, results may vary depending on the ingredients used.
Vinegar and alcohol reductions should be done over medium heat, though the most important thing is that the chosen pan only have direct contact with the heat in its base. If the flames reach the edges of the pan, they can burn the product, causing it to stick to the sides as it reduces. This alters the resulting flavor and causes small black particles to form which do not disappear even after straining the reduction.

Balsamic vinegar reduction

Ingredients

- 26-1/2 oz. balsamic vinegar

Method

1. Heat the 26-1/2 oz. of balsamic vinegar in a saucepan and reduce to 2/3 cup.

Forum vinegar reduction

Ingredients

- 26-1/2 oz. Forum* vinegar

Method

1. Heat the 26-1/2 oz. of Forum vinegar in a saucepan and reduce to 2/3 cup.

Wine and Soy Reduction

Ingredients

- 1-1/2 cup sweet sherry (dark)
- 1-1/2 cup red wine
- 3 tbsp. soy sauce

Method

1. Mix the two wines in a saucepan and reduce over heat to 2/3 cup.
2. Mix in the soy sauce while hot.

Hot and cold sauces

White brine

Ingredients

- 28 oz. olive oil
- 7 oz. white vinegar
- 1/2 garlic head
- 2 bay leaves
- 1 twig fresh thyme
- 4 black peppercorns
- 1 onion, julienned
- 14 oz. bouillon

Method

1. Stew all of the ingredients except the vinegar and bouillon over low heat.
2. Add half of the vinegar and stock and raise the heat for a few minutes.
3. Remove from heat and slowly pour in the rest of the vinegar until you obtain the desired flavor.

Note: this brine must be stirred before use because the vinegar sinks to the bottom.

White truffle mayonnaise

Ingredients

- 1/2 cup white truffle (*Tuber magnatum*) oil
- 2 egg yolks
- 1-1/3 tbsp. mineral water
- salt

Method

1. Use the same method as that for conventional mayonnaise.

Butter pesto

Ingredients

- 2 oz. fresh basil
- 2 tsp. dried garlic cloves
- 2 oz. pine nuts
- 3-1/2 oz. finely grated parmesan
- 3-1/2 oz. clarified butter
- salt and pepper

Method

1. Wash and completely dry the basil leaves.
2. Blanch the garlic in boiling water for a few seconds and cool.
3. Blend all of the ingredients together except for the clarified butter.
4. Emulsify the resulting paste with the clarified butter (make sure that there remain no clumps and it has uniform color). Store at 37°F (3°C).

Salmorejo* sauce
(without marinating the rabbit meat)

Ingredients

- 3/4 qt. white wine
- 1/4 qt. red wine vinegar
- 1/4 qt. olive oil
- 15 garlic cloves
- 1/2 tsp. de freshly ground black pepper
- 1/2 tsp. ground chili pepper
- 1/2 tsp. paprika
- 1 pinch thyme leaves
- 1 pinch oregano leaves
- coarse grain salt
- bones and trimmings (obtained from de-boning two rabbits)
- brown stock

METHOD

1. Mash the garlic with the salt and pepper to make a paste. Add the chili pepper and paprika.
2. Add the wine and vinegar. Gradually pour in the oil while stirring to emulsify and make a smooth sauce.
3. Move the mixture to a saucepan and add the thyme and oregano. Mix in the rabbit bones and trimmings and allow to marinate.
4. Lightly brown the marinated bones and trimmings.
5. Roast them in the oven. Once removed and while still very hot, stir the rabbit bones and trimmings once again into the saucepan with the marinade.
6. Cover with brown stock and simmer over low heat for 2 hours.
7. Very finely strain.

ROMESCO* SAUCE (MILD)

INGREDIENTS

- 12 lightly toasted almonds
- 12 lightly toasted hazelnuts
- 12 lightly toasted pine nuts
- 2 small fried bread slices
- 1 roasted garlic clove
- 1/2 raw garlic clove
- 1 roasted tomato
- 1 *romesco* pepper or 2 dried red peppers (blanched with their skin)
- ground black pepper
- olive oil (for emulsifying)
- vinegar
- salt

METHOD

1. Combine and blend all of the ingredients, slowly adding the oil until emulsified.
2. Place in a chinois and continue to blend with a hand-held blender.
3. Refrigerate.
4. Once cold, emulsify once again and adjust salt, vinegar and oil quantities to taste.
5. If you prefer it spicier, cautiously add ground cayenne pepper.

Note: a fisherman gave my father this recipe. Of course, he did not use a strainer and only served it with fish dishes. My opinion is that it can be served with everything except desserts (as of yet).

Tomato paste

Ingredients

- 2-3/16 lbs. ripe tomatoes on the vine

Method

1. Wash the tomatoes, halve them and remove the seeds.
2. Grate them by hand with a grater over a strainer or sieve.
3. Leave for 3 hours minimum in the refrigerator with a bowl underneath to drain the water.

Note: this process separates the water from the pulp.
The recipes in this book use only the pulp, although I recommend never throwing out the water from the tomatoes—after a few hours of sedimentation we obtain a clear liquid with a delicious flavor of pure tomato and many possibilities for use.

Purées, fillings, mousses and pastes

Béchamel for croquettes

Ingredients

- 1 qt. fresh milk
- 5-3/8 oz. flour
- 4-3/8 oz. butter
- 4 hard-boiled eggs, grated (about 5 oz.)
- salt

Method

1. Melt the butter over low heat and add the flour. Whisk to make a thick cream.
2. Without removing from heat and while still whisking, slowly mix in the milk.
3. Once all of the milk is incorporated, keep over heat for a few minutes while beating vigorously.
4. Add the grated eggs to the béchamel as uniformly as possible so that it does not concentrate in isolated spots. Season.

Note: this béchamel is a filling. To use it as a sauce, use only half the flour, leave out the eggs and run it through the Thermomix at the highest speed with heat.

Béchamel bolognese

Ingredients

- 24-1/2 oz. béchamel for croquettes (p. 198)
- 10-1/2 oz. Bolognese sauce

Method

1. Drain as much of the oil as possible from the Bolognese sauce (I recommend doing this while hot).
2. Mix the two sauces while hot, then refrigerate.

Note: Never mix the two sauces with an electric blender because the béchamel will lose its consistency.

Béchamel carbonara

Ingredients

- 24-1/2 oz. béchamel for croquettes (p. 198)
- 10-1/2 oz. Carbonara sauce

Method

1. Mix the two sauces while hot, then refrigerate.

Note: Never mix the two sauces with an electric blender because the béchamel will lose its consistency.

Four cheese béchamel

Ingredients

- 24-1/2 oz. béchamel for croquettes (p. 198)
- 10-1/2 oz. thick four cheese sauce
  (this is no more than a blend of your four cheeses of choice; one of which should always be a blue cheese, e.g. Cabrales, Gorgonzola, Roquefort, etc.)

Method

1. Mix the two sauces while hot.

Note: Never mix the two sauces with an electric blender because the béchamel will lose its consistency.
If the cheeses release fat in liquid form, stir when it is almost cold to blend it in.

Béchamel napolitana

Ingredients

- 24-1/2 oz. béchamel for croquettes (p. 198)
- 10-1/2 oz. tomato sauce
- oregano

Method

1. Drain as much of the oil as possible from the tomato sauce (I recommend doing this while still hot).
2. Mix the two sauces while hot.
3. Add oregano to taste.

Note: Never mix the two sauces with an electric blender because the béchamel will lose its consistency.

Pesto béchamel

Ingredients

- 24-1/2 oz. béchamel for croquettes (p. 198)
- 10-1/2 oz. butter *pesto*

Method

1. Mix the two sauces while hot.

Note: Never mix the two sauces with an electric blender because the béchamel will lose its consistency.

Miso purée

Ingredients

- 14 oz. cream
- 4-1/2 oz. white *miso** paste
- 1 gelatin sheet

Method

1. Soak the gelatin in plenty of water.
2. Drain and place in a saucepan over medium heat.
3. Add some of the cream and blend well.
4. Add the *miso* and the remaining cream. Stir until homogeneous.
5. Refrigerate for 12 hours. Emulsify.

Green tea paste

Ingredients

- 1 tbsp. powdered green tea (ceremonial variety)
- 24-1/2 oz. cream
- 1-3/4 oz. sugar
- 2 gelatin sheets

Method

1. Soak the gelatin in plenty of cold water.
2. Boil the cream with the powdered green tea and the sugar.
3. Drain the gelatin and heat in a saucepan.
4. Once melted, add part of the cream, green tea and sugar mixture. Stir well.
5. Mix in the rest of the mixture and refrigerate.
6. After a minimum of 4 hours, emulsify.

Finely chopped grilled vegetables and blood sausage

Ingredients

- 10-1/2 oz. grilled vegetables
- 2 oz. Porcini mushrooms *(Boletus edulis)*, fresh or frozen
- 3 oz. blood sausage
- oil
- salt

Method

1. With a knife, very finely chop the vegetables (previously fire-grilled).
2. Sauté the mushrooms, cut into large dice, in a non-stick pan with a little oil until golden brown. Chop them as with the vegetables.
3. Crumble the blood sausage.
4. Sauté the vegetables, mushrooms and blood sausage together with a bit of oil, stirring occasionally.
5. Refrigerate until use.

Pumpkin purée

Ingredients

- 24-1/2 oz. pumpkin pulp
- 24-1/2 oz. butter
- 6-3/4 fl. cream
- salt

Method

1. Cook the pumpkin in the oven wrapped in aluminum foil or sous-vide in a steam oven.
2. Purée with the butter and cream.
3. Bring to a boil for a few minutes.
4. Refrigerate.

Note: there is canned pumpkin purée available on the market (certain brands are of quite respectable quality) that can save time and work.

Cauliflower purée

Ingredients

- 1 cauliflower
- 2 qt. milk
- 3 oz. butter
- salt

Method

1. Clean, cut and wash the cauliflower.
2. Bring the milk to a boil and add the cauliflower.
3. Once cooked, drain, keeping the milk. Place the cauliflower with the butter into the Thermomix. Salt to taste.
4. Purée at high speed with heat and add part of the milk if necessary. Allow to cool.

Cheese and mint filling

Ingredients

- 14 oz. dense fresh cheese, drained
- 3-1/2 oz. butter
- 2 garlic cloves, finely chopped (about 1-1/2 tsp.)
- 1 bunch fresh mint, finely chopped

Method

1. Purée all of the ingredients to make a smooth, homogenous mixture.
2. Refrigerate.

Miscellaneous recipes

Stewing oil

Ingredients

- 1 pint olive oil
- 1 pint sunflower oil
- 1 garlic clove with peel
- 10 black peppercorns
- 1 bay leaf
- salt

Method

1. Combine all of the ingredients.

Note: this oil does not need to marinate before use—it will become flavored due to the heat during the stewing process.

Simple syrup

Ingredients

- 1-1/16 qt. water
- 1-2/16 lb. sugar

Method

1. Place the sugar and water mixture in a saucepan over heat. Stir.
2. Bring to a boil, then remove from heat and allow to cool.
3. Refrigerate in a covered container.

Note: Simple syrup is made with 50% water, 50% sugar. If you prefer a less sweet syrup, the proportions can be adjusted to 1-1/16 qt. of water and half the quantity of sugar.

Dough for frying

Ingredients

- 10-1/2 oz. flour
- 1 tsp. sugar
- 1/2 tsp. salt
- 1 tsp. pressed yeast
- 1 lb. water (approx.)
- ice

Method

1. Warm some of the water and dissolve the yeast in it.
2. Mix in the remaining ingredients.
3. Allow to ferment for about 3 hours.
4. Add ice just before use.

GLOSSARY

CALDERETA: a typical Spanish dish common to virtually all regions of the country, taking its name from the pot traditionally used to prepare it (the *caldera*). There are various types: lamb (the *manchega*, from Castilla-La Mancha, or the *extremeña*, from Extremadura), veal, or seafood *calderetas*... One of the most well-known and delicious is the lobster *caldereta*, with long tradition in the Balearic Islands.

CARQUINYOLI: small very crunchy candy typically found in some small Catalan towns. Made with sugar, flour, eggs and mainly toasted almonds.

ESCUDELLA I CARN D'OLLA: name of a traditional Catalan stew.

FORUM VINEGAR: high quality sweet and sour cabernet-sauvignon wine vinegar produced at the El Vendrell winery (in the Tarragona province, northeastern Spain).

GORDAL OLIVE: large meaty olive, much larger in size than other varieties.

KONBU SEEWEED: very important seeweed in Japanese cooking, used to flavor stocks and to prepare sushi rice. Sold dry in strips, characterized by a light powder covering it that must be removed before use.

NEUTRAL GLAZE: flavorless gelatin with a gel texture that can be applied without heating it.

NORI SEEWEED: thin dark green seeweed sold in dried sheets. It has one side shinier than the other, and when it absobs moisture it darkens in color to become almost black.

MAKISU: small mat made with thin bamboo rods used to roll Japanese rice rolls called maki.

MICRI: neutral vegetable base that is virtually colorless, tasteless and odorless. Invented by Miguel Sánchez Romera, owner and chef of L´Esguard de Llavaneras restaurant in Barcelona, Spain. Will blend and thicken any liquid, with or without heat. It accents its shine, color and aromas, while at the same time giving consistency for sauces and liquids without affecting its main characteristics. Micri can be obtained from specialized vendors.

MIRIN: liquid sweetener. Made by adding distilled alcohol to steamed rice with gluten. After 40-60 days, it yields a sweet liquid with about 14% alcohol. It is used in cooking, mainly in making sushi rice.

MISO: paste made from fermented soy germ, to which is added either barley or rice and salt. A basic ingredient in Japanese cuisine used mainly as a condiment to enhance flavors. There are various types: red, white and even sweet. Miso soup is one of the mainstays of Japanese cuisine.

OSHIZUSHI: actually oshizushi gata. An odd little rectangular box with a cover and removable base into which rice is pressed. It has slits to facilitate slicing pieces for sushi.

PITAHAYA: refreshing and aromatic fruit similar to the chumbo fig cultivated mainly in Colombia. There are two types: yellow, with a spiny peel and white pulp; and red, with a thinner peel and a carmine red color, less aromatic than the first.

ROMESCO: very popular Catalan sauce served mainly with fish. Every household prepares it differently, but the recipes always include chopped nuts, bread and garlic, tomato, olive oil and the requisite romesco peppers (dry red peppers).

SALMOREJO, RABBIT WITH: dish typical of the Canary Islands. Not to be confused with "salmorejo", a cold soup similar to gazpacho originating in Córdoba (Andalucía).

SOMEN: very thin Japanese buckwheat noodles.

STEW: to cook in oil at low temperatures without letting it boil (this term has other meanings in cooking, but this is the one used in this book).

SUQUET: traditional dish made by the fishermen of Catalonia, the Balearic Islands and Valencia. It consists of a fish stew slow-cooked in a light broth; the traditional recipe calls for certain key elements, but there are no strict rules as to the types of fish used. This freedom with ingredients characterizes the dish: one could say that there are as many varieties of *suquet* as there are types of fish on the coast.

TORTA DE LA SERENA: hand-made regional cheese made with merino sheep's milk. It is pressed, refined, with high fat content and very creamy. It has the texture of fondue, only cold (it is liquid at room temperature). A brilliant ivory in color, covered in a yellowish ochre crust presenting the peculiar wrapping stamp (a strip of braided grass). Its flavor is unequaled, with a delicious and intense sheep milk aroma. It is made in Badajoz (Spain) with admirable craft.

Acknowledgements

To my parents and sisters (Botella González Family)

To my wife, Carmen

The Fernández Hernández Family

Víctor Sánchez

Manel Huete

Juan Manuel Clavero

Txema Salvans

Víctor Oller

The Huete Ferriz Family

Romy Balaguer

Lorenzo Milá

Xavi Mill

Víctor Sabater

Anna Guirado

Armando Béjar

Néstor Padial

Ramon Saltó

Eric Besse

Viçens Arias

The Alemany Mascareñas Family

Joan Piqué and Cristina

Llorenç Petràs

Solé – Graells

Mª Rosa of Suministros Girona

Ingrid Bordas

Costals Family

Industrias IMA of Figueras

Montse Costals
Francisco Marfull
Fco. Javier Antoja
Cèlia Pujals
René Palomo
Carmen Celdrán
Montagud Editores
Xavier Corretjé
Miguel Sánchez Romera
Sardaukar (Production facility of Grupo Paradís)
Mr. Norton of "La Bolera" restaurant in Canyet (Barcelona, Spain)
C.B.G. (Ripoll – Girona, Spain)
Mas Tubert (Camprodón – Girona, Spain)
Sandro Desii
The entire staff of El Bulli
Juan Vinyas of the "La llar de Roses" restaurant in Roses (Girona, Spain)
Pere Pou and Teresa Bofill of Empordà Seleccions

A very special mention to Ramón Marín Marín, who left us this year and is undoubtedly part of this book

BIBLIOGRAPHY

ADRIÀ, Albert
Los postres de El Bulli
Ediciones Península. Barcelona, 1998

ADRIÀ, Ferran
El Bulli. El sabor del Mediterráneo
Editorial Antártida / Empúries. Barcelona, 1993

BALAGUER, Oriol
La cocina de los postres
Montagud Editores. Barcelona, 2001
Dessert Cuisine
Montagud Editores. Barcelona, 2002

LLADONOSA I GIRÓ, Josep
El gran libro de la cocina catalana
Ediciones Península. Barcelona, 1991

TAKAGI, Kayoko, Shuji SHIONO
El arte de la cocina japonesa
Tf. Editores. Madrid, 1997

Original title: *Cocina para Cóctel*
First published in 2002 by Montagud Editores, S.A.

Ausiàs March, 25, 1º
08010 Barcelona. Spain.
Tel.: + 34 933 18 20 82
Fax: +34 933 02 50 83
e-mail: montagud@montagud.com
www.montagud.com

Filmsetting: PC Fotocomposición, S.A.
Printing: Castuera, Industrias Gráficas, S.A.

Copyright Registration: NA1654/2007
ISBN: 978-84-7212-104-1